BECOMING A BETTER TUTOR

A Data-Driven Approach to Tutoring

2nd Edition

Dr. Alicia Holland, EdD

Book Titles by Dr. Alicia Holland

Dr. Alicia Holland's
Becoming a Better Tutor:
A Data-Driven Approach to Tutoring

Book 1:
Expanding Your Tutoring Business:
*The Blueprint for Building a
Global Learning Organization*

Book 2:
Expanding Your Tutoring Business:
*The Blueprint for Hiring Tutors and Independent
Contractors*

Book 3:
Dr. Alicia Holland's
Expanding Your Tutoring Business:
*The Blueprint for Protecting
Your Learning Organization*

Dr. Alicia Holland's
**Starting and Operating an
Online Tutoring Business:**
*The Blueprint for Running an
Online Learning Organization*

Note: Check Dr. Alicia Holland's Personal Website
for her latest work at
www.dr-holland.com

BECOMING A BETTER TUTOR

A Data-Driven Approach to Tutoring

2nd Edition

Dr. Alicia Holland, EdD

All rights reserved. No parts of this book may be used or reproduced by any means, graphic, electronic, or mechanical, including photocopying, recording, taping or by any information storage retrieval system without the written permission of the author except in the case of brief quotations embodied in critical articles and reviews.

This book may be ordered through booksellers or by contacting:

iGlobal Educational Services, LLC
PO Box 7404
Round Rock, Texas 78683-7404
www.iglobaleducation.com
512-761-5898

Because of the dynamic nature of the Internet, any web addresses or links contained in this book may have changed since publication and may no longer be valid. The views expressed in this work are solely those of the author and do not necessarily reflect the views of the publisher, and the publisher hereby disclaims any responsibility for them.

Copyright ©2010 through 2013 by Dr. Alicia Holland, EdD

All rights reserved.

ISBN: 0988227142

ISBN-13: 978-0-9882271-4-9

Dedication

This book is dedicated to my parents, Nathan and Vera Holland, my maternal grandmother, Georgia Brumfield Johnson, and my paternal grandfather, Percy Holland. I also would like to dedicate this book to my spiritual uncle, Matthew Murray. I know that you are extremely proud of me. Although you are in heaven, I felt your presence while working on this important chapter of my life. I will always remember the life lessons and pearls of wisdom that you shared with me. I love each of you dearly and hope to see you all again someday.

To Georgia, Amaiya, and future children, I dedicate this to you, too! I want you to know that you can do whatever you desire as long as you have God and a good support system in your corner. You are blessed, and I want you to know that you were my motivation for completing this book. I love you!

Table of Contents

How this Book is Organized 1
About the Author 5
Acknowledgments 7
Introduction 9
About this Book 11
My Assumptions 13

PART I: The Early Stages of Planning Your Tutoring Business

CHAPTER 1: Introduction to the
Fabulous World of Tutoring 17
    Why Tutoring Is in Demand *17*
    Professional Tutoring Associations *18*
    Who Can Tutor *23*
    Assessing Your Strengths and Weaknesses *27*
    Finding Your Niche and Predicting
       Your Chances for Success *30*
    Crafting Your Professional Tutor's Résumé *31*

CHAPTER 2: Starting Up and Legalizing
Your Tutoring Business 34
    Developing a Tutoring Philosophy *34*
    Developing Vision and Mission Statements *36*
    The Importance of a Business Plan *40*
    Obtaining the Business License and
       Business Checking Account *40*

Determining the Location and
  Hours of Operation 41
The Tutoring Environment 45
Developing Business Forms for
  Your Tutoring Business 49

PART II: Establishing and Promoting Your Tutoring Business

CHAPTER 3: Effectively Attracting Clients to Your Tutoring Business 58
  Basic Marketing Strategies 60
  Advanced Marketing Strategies 62
  E-mail Advertising 62
  Getting a Website Started 63

CHAPTER 4: Pricing to Win: A Choice That Will Make or Break Your Tutoring Business 69
  Understanding Your Tutoring Prices 69
  Researching Your Tutoring Competition 71
  Evaluating Your Potential Clients 73
  Applying Pricing Strategies That Lead to Sales 74

PART III: Taking Care of Your Tutoring Business

CHAPTER 5: Keeping Track of Your Money 78
  Establishing Good Credit and Fixing Bad Credit 79
  Understanding Cash Flow 82
  Using Your Tutoring Schedule 82
  Deciding on an Accounting System 83
  Basic Bookkeeping for Your Tutoring Business 83

CHAPTER 6: Staying on Top When Business Is Down 87
  Maintaining a Good Relationship with Clients 87
  Following Up with Clients Regularly 88
  Handling Conflicts and Nonpayment 90
  Finding Ways to Cut Expenses 91

Offering Special Promotions 95
Client Referral System 95
Finding Opportunities to Supplement
   Your Tutoring Income 97
Teaching and Tutoring Online 97

PART IV: Data-Driven Strategies for Tutoring

CHAPTER 7: Tutoring Consultations and How to Handle Them 106
Who Are Your Best Clients? 107
Mastering Tutoring Interviews and
   Tutoring Consultations 109

CHAPTER 8: Conducting the Needs Assessment and Developing Instructional Plans 117
How to Conduct a Needs Assessment for
   Your Tutoring Business 117
How to Identify Your Clients' Needs 120
Interview Questions for Parents 121
Using Pre- and Post-Assessments with Your Clients 123
Using Licensed Pre- and Post-Assessments to
   Measure Student Progress 123
Developing the Instructional Plan 125
Progress-Monitoring Assessments in Tutoring 126
Setting Goals in Tutoring 127

CHAPTER 9: Determining the Type of Tutor You Will Need to Be for Each Tutoring Session 133
Homework Tutor 134
Instructional Tutor 137
Strategic Tutor 139
Tutoring Archetypes That Work Best with
   High School and Adult Learners 142
The Pragmatist Tutor 143
The Architect Tutor 145
The Surveyor Tutor 148

CHAPTER 10: Conducting Tutoring Sessions
and Writing Monitoring Notes for Client **148**
    The Tutoring Framework for Effective Tutoring *150*
    How to Open Tutoring Sessions *153*
    Sample Opening of a Tutoring Session *154*
    How to Close Tutoring Sessions *154*
    Sample Closing of a Tutoring Session *155*
    Structure of Tutoring Sessions *156*
    Praising Student Motivation and Performance in
        Tutoring Sessions *157*
    Reward Systems in Tutoring *160*
    Using the Tickets to Enhance Your Reward System in
        Your Tutoring Practice *161*
    Using Small Gifts and Gift Cards to Enhance
        Your Reward System in Your Tutoring Practice *163*
    Writing Monitoring Notes for Clients during
        Tutoring Sessions *165*
    Using Tutoring Session Time Cards for
        Tutoring Sessions *173*
    Providing Student's Additional Practice After
        Tutoring Sessions *174*

PART V: Taking Tutoring to the Classroom: Combining Classroom Teaching and Tutoring

CHAPTER 11: Tutoring Strategies:
A Way to Increase Student
Achievement in the Classroom **178**
    The Role of a Teacher as the Tutor in the Classroom *179*
    In-Class Tutoring Method *181*
    How Is In-Class Tutoring Structured? *181*
    Tracking Students' Progress during In-Class Tutoring *183*
    Peer Tutoring in the Classroom *185*
    Structure of Peer Tutoring in the Classroom *186*
    Using Online Tutoring in the Classroom *188*

References **191**

Appendices

APPENDIX A:
Sample Professional Tutoring Résumé 196

APPENDIX B:
Sample Tutoring Services Registration 200

APPENDIX C:
Sample Tutoring Services Registration 204

APPENDIX D:
Sample Tutoring Guidelines 207

APPENDIX E:
Sample Client Policies and Procedures 209

APPENDIX F:
Sample Instructional Plan 212

APPENDIX G:
Sample Monitoring Notes 214

APPENDIX H:
Sample Teacher's Online Tutoring 216

Index 217

How This Book is Organized

Becoming a Better Tutor: A Data-Driven Approach to Tutoring is organized into five major parts—the following sections explain what you will find in each part.

Part I: The Early Stages of Planning Your Tutoring Business

In this section, I introduce you to the fabulous world of tutoring. You will discover why tutoring is in high demand and who can enter the tutoring profession. You will also learn strategies that will help you plan for your tutoring business. In addition, I talk about the importance of a business plan and how to develop business forms for your tutoring business.

Part II: Establishing and Promoting Your Tutoring Business

The chapters in this section discuss the various marketing strategies to promote your tutoring business and start a website. There are a myriad of marketing strategies that can be used, but in this part, you will learn the best approaches to use for your tutoring business. I also give you ideas on how to price your services. You will then explore some questions that will help you understand how to set your tutoring rates.

Part III: Taking Care of Your Tutoring Business

Once you have started your tutoring business, you will need to take care of it. It's just like any other valuable item; you must protect and care for it. In this section, a chapter is dedicated to helping you understand cash flow and how to choose an accounting system. In addition, I discuss the importance of establishing good credit and fixing bad credit for the sake of your tutoring business. Remember, this is your investment, and you need to know how to protect it.

I also include a chapter that focuses on maintaining relationships with clients, finding ways to cut expenses, and creating opportunities to supplement your tutoring income.

Part IV: Data-Driven Strategies to Tutoring

In this part, you will learn how to find your best clients and conduct tutoring consultations. Once you have determined the client's needs, you need to determine the type of tutor you will need to be. A chapter is dedicated to exploring various tutoring prototypes and how they are used in tutoring sessions. Not to mention, you will get a chance to explore the tutoring framework for effective tutoring sessions. You will also learn how to develop instructional plans for your clients, conduct tutoring sessions, and write monitoring notes for clients.

Part V: Taking Tutoring to the Classroom: Combining Classroom Teaching and Tutoring

In this part, I explore the role of a teacher as a tutor in the classroom. I also discuss tutoring models that can be implemented either individually or in small groups. At the back of the book, I provide references and several appendices that can help you start and run your tutoring business.

Where to Go from Here

You can join our group at www.becomingabettertutorblog.com to gain exclusive content, reserve either group or personal tutor coaching sessions, network with like-minded tutors, and stay updated about various aspects of the tutoring industry.

I know that it can be extremely intimidating to leave your day job or think about starting your own business. It was hard for me, too, but I made the bold decision to supplement my income by tutoring. Once I realized the potential, I began educating myself and making plans to go full-time with my tutoring business, and you should do the same. I hope Becoming a Better Tutor: A Data-Driven Approach to Tutoring helps you achieve these goals and encourages you to maintain your commitment to starting your tutoring business and keeping the faith. You can do it!

About the Author

Dr. Alicia Holland is one of those rare people who can say she is an educator, professional tutor, instructional designer, curriculum developer, online professor, life coach, consultant, speaker, and author and mean it. She started her teaching career at the age of 20 and later earned her doctorate degree in Education from Nova Southeastern University in Ft. Lauderdale, Florida in 2010 at the age of 26. Her God-Given talents and skills have attracted clients such as school districts throughout the United States, state agencies, and other leading learning organizations, including in the private sector.

Dr. Holland consults with tutors and other learning organizations both large and small. Her tutoring blog for tutors has been online since 2010 and she coaches tutors around the world. Typically, she speaks at major conferences each year on topics in education, including tutoring. Dr. Holland is an online associate faculty member at Concordia University Portland where she teaches doctoral level organizational leadership and writing courses in the School of Education.

Also, Dr. Holland has held appointments as an online professor at Ashford University, American College of Education, and Everest Online where she served in the capacity of Internship Supervisor for Bilingual and English Language Learner Educators and taught various courses in Education, Life Skills and Critical Thinking. Additionally, at Capella University, in the Graduate School of Education, she taught various courses in Education and currently serves as a Dissertation Mentor for Doctoral Learners. Lastly, Dr. Holland teaches doctoral level research courses and serve as either Dissertation Chair or Committee Member at the University of Phoenix. Currently, she is serving as a Lead Area Faculty Chair in Research and was awarded and recognized as one of the 2016 Research Fellows for her research on *Meditation, Mindfulness, and Critical Thinking*. In July 2017, Dr. Holland and her research team will present the original research at Ryerson University in Toronto, Canada.

Outside of Academia, Dr. Holland is a Transformational, Intuitive Life Coach and Ordained Spiritual Minister. In September 2016, she presented her personal development presentation, *Changing Your Client's Story through Personal Power* at Harvard University in Boston, Massachusetts. In November 2017, Dr. Alise will be in Paris, France (City of Love & Freedom) sharing research on *"Integrating Flower Essences Therapy and Intuition in Life Coaching"* at the 8th International Conference on Traditional & Alternative Medicine.

When Dr. Holland is not developing new content, life coaching, tutoring, teaching, or consulting with her clients, you can usually find her sight-seeing and spending quality time with her family enjoying the Desert Sunrises and Sunsets.

Acknowledgments

First, I want to thank God for helping me realize my purpose in life and keeping me on track when, at times, I wanted to stray. Thanks to my loving husband, Corey, for encouraging me to stay focused and watching our two young daughters, Georgia and Amaiya, while I worked on this book.

Also, I want to thank George Nedef for his pearls of wisdom and helping me learn the publishing side of writing a book; there are no words to thank you for your leadership.

Introduction

Maybe you're a teacher looking to supplement your income. Maybe you're a homemaker looking to make extra money or a recent graduate having a tough time in today's job market. Whatever your circumstances, this book will help you learn about starting, running, and succeeding with your own tutoring business. This book will also help you realize that tutoring requires an open mind and other actions than running a small business in a different industry.

Starting your own tutoring business can be very scary. I know this from both a professional and a personal point of view. You probably have a working knowledge of tutoring, but you need good information to help you with the decisions ahead, and my goal with this book is to provide you with this information. I believe that my perspective, as someone who owns and operates her own tutoring business and has an extensive amount of experience in the education industry, can help you.

About This Book

I have two primary goals with this book. First, I want to explain what tutoring is and how it has become a billion-dollar industry; and second, my goal is to guide you in the process of starting and running your tutoring business.

You don't have to read this book chronologically from the first page to the last—although you can. You may want to read the first chapter to get an understanding of the tutoring industry and then move to the chapters that cater to your needs.

My Assumptions

In order to provide you with material to meet your unique tutoring needs, I had to make some basic assumptions. I assume the following:

1. You have a desire to start a tutoring business or are already in business.
2. You want information on how to start and run your tutoring business successfully.
3. You know how to work with children and adults.

Part I:
The Early Stages of Planning Your Tutoring Business

CHAPTER 1:
Introduction to the Fabulous World of Tutoring

I n this chapter, you will:
- Learn why tutoring is in high demand and why parents choose specific tutors.
- Read about the different types of professional tutoring associations.
- Discover the many people who enter the tutoring profession.
- Assess your strengths and weaknesses to help determine your tutoring niche.
- Find your niche and predict your chances for success as a tutor.
- Craft your professional tutor's résumé.

Why Tutoring Is in Demand

"Tutoring is a huge industry in much of Asia and is growing fast elsewhere, particularly in Africa, Europe, and North America," (Bray and Silova, 2006, p. 516). Tutoring is in demand because it's no secret that many children are having problems grasping concepts in class. This can be linked to a variety of factors, including high teacher/student ratio and peer pressure. In addition, many educators do not have the time or energy to help students after school. Bottom line? Parents are highly concerned about their children's futures and will seek the help that they need in academics.

In today's society, many parents are realizing that they truly have control over their children's education and that many options are available to them to supplement their education. This is where you come into the picture. Oftentimes parents turn to private tutors (or tutoring companies) for assistance.

Another reason that tutoring is in demand is the bipartisan No Child Left behind (NCLB) Act that the United States Congress passed in 2001. The legislation promised high standards, accountability, more choices for parents, and research-based methods of instruction. According to Find a Franchise.com (2010), "When the NCLB Act became the law of the land, the tutoring industry quickly exploded into a staggering four billion dollar business," (para. 4). This opened up new opportunities for people from many walks of life, but it also created the sense that tutors (or tutoring companies) were to be held accountable, along with parents, teachers, administrators, and other key stakeholders in the educational system.

As the tutoring industry was growing exponentially, so did the need for professional tutoring associations. In the next section, we will explore the different types of professional tutoring associations.

Professional Tutoring Associations

In any profession, professional associations are necessary for providing a safe haven for professionals to learn and grow. Well, this type of professionalism did not occur in the tutoring profession until 1990. After 1990, several worthy tutoring associations formed and have gained respect in the tutoring industry. Let's look at the tutoring associations that were formed toward the end of the twentieth century. These associations were the Association of Educators in Private Practice (AEPP) and the National Tutoring Association.

Association of Educators in Private Practice (AEPP)

The first tutoring association, founded in 1990, was named the Association of Educators in Private Practice (AEPP). This organization was renamed the Education Industry Association (EIA) in 2002, because the organization wanted to include the variety of enterprises that were providing market-based services. Now, the EIA has over eight hundred corporate and individual members. Thus, it is considered the leading professional association for private providers of education services, suppliers, and other private organizations who are stakeholders in education (EIA, 2010).

National Tutoring Association (NTA)

Just two years later (1992), the second tutoring association, the National Tutoring Association (NTA), made its debut. According to the NTA, this association was formed for the following purpose: "To establish a membership organization for tutoring professionals" (NTA, 2010). In fact, the National Tutoring Association is the largest professional association dedicated exclusively to tutoring. NTA represents the interests of more than 16,000 tutors in the U.S. and 7 other countries, practicing in all phases of tutoring, program administration, and supplemental student services. Members represent colleges, universities, high schools, middle schools, elementary schools, school districts, literacy programs, community programs, grant supported programs, and NCLB/SES providers. Also, NTA welcomes peer, paraprofessional, professional, volunteer, and private practice tutors (NTA, 2010, para. 3).

This organization has been around for more than two decades and has made many positive contributions to the tutoring profession. On the brink of the twenty-first century and the era of No Child Left behind (NCLB), several other tutoring associations were established. These tutoring associations include the American Tutoring Association, the Association for the Tutoring Profession, and the International Tutoring Association.

The American Tutoring Association and the International Tutoring Association

The third association, the American Tutoring Association (ATA), was formed in 2000. This organization is a 501(c)(3) nonprofit organization dedicated to creating excellence in private tutoring (ATA, 2010). This organization provides tutoring certification and credibility as a private tutor. In 2006, Mark Greenwood formed the fifth tutoring association—the International Tutoring Association (ITA). This organization is intended to be a place for tutors to develop their professional talents and techniques.

Tutors are also encouraged to provide professional tips, exchange stories, and share resources (ITA, 2010). Not only does ITA cater to private tutors, but it also provides quality training to university-level programs.

Association for the Tutoring Profession

The Association for the Tutoring Profession (ATP) had its beginnings in 2003; it became ATP in 2004. This organization is not affiliated with any private sector and promotes scholarly research and professional experiences as a tutor in any tutoring setting (i.e., university, private, center-based, etc.) (ATP, 2010).

Now that you have been exposed to the many tutoring associations, are you wondering which association would best supply your needs as a private tutor? Well, let me share my professional experience and advice with you.

International Tutoring and Teaching Symposium

The International Tutoring and Teaching Symposium (ITTS) was formed back in 2016. This is an annual professional tutoring conference that is designed to serve tutors, educators, academic coaches, mentors, tutor business owners, and the supplemental educational service industry around the world. This conference is associated with iGlobal Educational Services and it promotes scholarly research and professional experiences as tutoring and educational practitioners in any educational setting.

> **EXPERT'S ADVICE:** The best advice that I can give to you is to make sure that your needs are being met at the professional tutoring association. In other words, if you are a private tutor, then you want to make sure that there are topics that can be applied to your specific situation. Otherwise, it may be best to focus on the specific content area in which you tutor and grow in that area.
>
> In an effort to assist you, please make sure that you answer the following questions prior to joining any professional association, especially in the tutoring industry.
>
> 1. What do you want out of the membership?
> 2. Are you looking for certification as a tutor? Which professional tutoring association offers the most benefits for your current and future needs?
> 3. How will joining this organization support your decision to tutor?

> **EXPERT'S ADVICE** *(continued)*
>
> These are the three questions that will guide you in making an appropriate decision about joining a tutoring association.

Types of Tutoring

There are various types of tutoring that can occur with learners. Specifically, there are two types of tutoring that can occur with learners that include both individualized tutoring and group tutoring. Both methods are effective for learners, but individuals really have to assess the learner's needs.

In addition, each method can be delivered either in-person in a physical environment or online in a virtual environment. The delivery method is also determined by the learner. Either method is effective.

Just like any other concept, there are advantages and disadvantages of both types of tutoring. Rather than list them out, let's compare the two types so you can make an informed decision on which method is better for your clients.

Individualized Tutoring Sessions	*Small Group Tutoring Sessions*
✧ Entire set time to interact with the tutor. ✧ One Learner. ✧ Same or Multiple Subjects.	✧ Limited time to interact with the tutor. ✧ 3-5 Learners. ✧ Same or Multiple Subjects.

Tutors will have to determine if they are ready to offer small group tutoring sessions. If learners are doing a great job in individual tutoring sessions, then it may be a great idea to continue conducting individualized tutoring sessions.

The bottom line is that both types of tutoring sessions are beneficial to learners, and tutors should conduct these sessions with the learner's best interest in mind.

Who Can Tutor

According to Merriam-Webster's online dictionary (2009), tutoring is "To teach or guide usually individually in a special subject or for a particular purpose," (para. 3). This definition does not restrict any individuals from tutoring. Thus, any person can tutor as long as he or she has both the knowledge and skills to be successful. Specifically, there are seven groups of people who may consider tutoring at some point in their lives. They are the following: (a) high school seniors; (b) college students; (c) degreed professionals; (d) professionals; (e) stay-at-home parents; (f) former military; and (g) retired individuals. Members of each of these groups bring a special set of skills to the tutoring profession. In my opinion, each group is qualified to tutor.

High School Seniors	College Students	Degreed Professionals
Professionals	Stay-At-Home Parents	Former Military
	Retired Individuals	

High school seniors are considered adults and are at the legal age where they can offer their services to their friends and/or family members. This allows both college and high school seniors to benefit from referrals and have the opportunity to work as private tutors. Similarly, college students offer their services to the same clientele as high school students, but they have the college experience and credits (at least eighteen hours) in the specific subject area they are tutoring, which is always an added benefit.

SCENARIO: "High School Ambitions"

Edward, a senior in high school, started helping his friends with calculus and trigonometry. In the summer, he got a tutoring gig at a local community program to work with students who needed help in these topics. Edward was hesitant about taking the gig, but he realized that there were no more offers on the table for a high school student. He could either take the position or be jobless for the summer. Several weeks later, Edward realized that he liked to tutor and would try to help others in the fall, either at the local community center or on his own at a local library.

1. Do you think that Edward made the right decision? Why or why not?

_____

_____

_____

_____

2. What type of advice would you give Edward regarding tutoring since he is starting so young?

_____
_____
_____
_____
_____

Degreed professionals are individuals who hold a bachelor's, master's, or doctorate degree in academia. They typically generalize in a certain area and are considered experts specifically for their program of study. On the other hand, college students are either traditional or nontraditional students working toward a degree; they are typically flexible with their tutoring schedules. Oftentimes these students pick up a range of skills working various jobs and as a result, they are able to relate well to their clients. This group could include substitute teachers as well.

Professionals and stay-at-home parents are people who may or may not hold a degree but have a great deal of experience in a certain subject or area. This qualifies them to tutor others in their specialty areas, such as chemistry, physics, or foreign languages. Stay-at-home parents may opt to offer tutoring services to others for a nominal fee while homeschooling their own children.

Former military and retired individuals may choose to tutor others as a way to stay current with their knowledge while helping others. Members of these two groups make great tutors because of the life experiences they have had and the many different places they have seen throughout their lives. Because tutoring is not a "sit and get" method, these individuals can help clients relate specific content to the real world and apply it to their own lives.

SCENARIO: "Serving a Higher Purpose"

Leon, a former navy petty officer, decided to put his leadership and science skills to use. He applied to a local Craigslist posting about tutoring a tenth grader in organic chemistry and got the position. Immediately, he and the tenth grader met at a local coffee shop, which became their permanent spot to meet. Rather than working for a tutoring company, he decided that he would start up his own small tutoring business, given that he already possessed the necessary leadership skills to run a business and be an effective leader. Leon thought to himself, "I am still serving my country one person at a time." Imagine that!

1. Do you know of anyone who followed Leon's footsteps as a tutor? What type of advice would you seek from him or her?

_____
_____
_____
_____
_____

2. What was your reaction to Leon's own self-discovery of his purpose—"I am still serving my country one person at a time"?

_____
_____
_____
_____
_____

Assessing Your Strengths and Weaknesses

Are you considering a tutoring career? Before you can tutor, you need to answer a few questions so you can become aware of what you really want from a tutoring career and what skills you need to do so.

Please write down your answers to the following questions.

   1. How much teaching and/or tutoring have you done so far?

   _____
   _____
   _____
   _____
   _____

   2. Which subjects did you teach and/or tutor (be specific— Elementary Math, Algebra I, Spanish II)?

   _____
   _____
   _____
   _____
   _____

   3. What kinds of professional development classes, college courses, or workshops (that specifically focus on tutoring) have you taken? List and give details about each of them.

   _____
   _____
   _____
   _____

4. Describe your education. Do you have any degree(s) or advanced degree(s)? Are you a certified teacher?

_____
_____
_____
_____
_____

5. Do you belong to any professional organizations, including professional tutoring organizations? If so, list them.

_____
_____
_____
_____
_____

6. What experience do you have with technology? Do you have a fax machine? Do you have a website or a blog?

_____
_____
_____
_____
_____

7. What do you think are your strengths as a tutor? What are your weaknesses? Explain.

_____
_____
_____
_____
_____

8. How well do you work with others? Explain.

_____
_____
_____
_____

9. How supportive is/are your significant other or family members of your tutoring career? Explain.

_____
_____
_____
_____

10. Do you have any experience in customer service? If so, list your experience.

_____
_____
_____
_____

11. How often do you set personal goals for yourself? Do you achieve these goals? Why or why not?

_____
_____
_____
_____

12. How would you rate yourself, on a scale of one to ten with one being the lowest and ten being the highest, with time management and organization? Why?

_____
_____
_____
_____
_____

13. How much money would you like to eventually make each year from tutoring? How much money do you need to start making right away from your tutoring business? Explain in detail.

_____
_____
_____
_____
_____

Your responses to these questions will help you assess your strengths and weaknesses. Also, they will help you discover the skills you already have to make your tutoring business successful (or the ones you lack).

Finding Your Niche and Predicting Your Chances for Success

If you took time to answer the previous questions, you probably discovered some things about yourself that gave you specific areas to work on in building your tutoring business. Maybe you realized that tutoring requires more dedication than you thought and that you may need to take additional academic classes to hone your tutoring skills and content knowledge.

In the next few weeks (or months), you should develop an action plan to improve these areas, prior to opening your tutoring business. In addition, you should have enough information to create a tutoring résumé.

Crafting Your Professional Tutor's Résumé

A résumé for a professional tutor should be succinct but informative.

Prospective clients want to skim a résumé to find the most important qualities they feel are necessary for a tutor. As with any other résumé, you want to make sure that you include the following sections: (1) education; (2) teaching and/or tutoring certifications; (3) first aid, AED, or CPR certifications; (4) teaching/tutoring experience; (5) skill set; (6) professional organizations; and (7) references.

Here are the reasons these components are important.

Education	Teaching, and/or tutoring certifications	First Aid, AED, or CPR Certifications
Teaching/Tutoring Experience	Skill Set	Professional Organizations
	References	

Education

First of all, your educational level lets the prospective clients know that you have the content knowledge and motivation to further your studies. For example, if you are a college student with a certain number of hours in a specific content area, then you would be highly qualified to tutor that specific area based upon your education and practical experience working with that content area.

Teaching and/or Tutoring Certifications

Your certifications also serve as a quick assessment of whether you are qualified in the areas in which prospective clients are seeking your services.

First Aid/AED (Automated External Defibrillator)/CPR Certification

This certification should be considered with all clients, but especially if you are considering working with clients who have special needs. Some clients will only choose tutors who have this type of certification, so it's definitely worth pursuing.

Teaching/Tutoring Experience

Prospective clients want to know if you have the necessary experience to work with them or their child. Therefore, for both teaching and tutoring experiences, please list out the various types of learners in which you have worked with to showcase that you have experience working with diverse learners.

Skill Set

Your skill set will showcase the qualities that you offer to your clients. This includes characteristics like being positive, flexible, organized, emotionally intelligent, and technology savvy and having strong interpersonal skills. By listing your skill set, you save time in the interview.

Just so that you know, parents will test you to see if these characteristics are present, and if they are (or are not), it will show during the interview or consultation.

Professional Associations

Your involvement in professional associations will show that you are "in the know" about state-of-the-art and research-based methods. Also, it shows that you are a lifelong learner.

References

Your references can be considered the lifeblood of your tutoring business; they can either make or break it. By listing your tutoring references, you will show that you are confident in your services and are valued as a tutor. Please be cautious about putting "Available upon request" on your résumé. This can be seen as having a negative connotation, which means you are too confident (arrogant) or may be hiding something. So, it's important to make sure you have at least three references; they should be three satisfied clients who have received three different services from you (i.e., test prep, math, and reading tutoring).

In this chapter, you learned why tutoring is in high demand and who could enter the tutoring profession. You were also able to assess your own strengths and weaknesses to find your tutoring niche, as well as revamp your résumé as a professional tutor. Are you ready for your own tutoring business? Well, it's time to explore how to start and legalize your tutoring business.

CHAPTER 2:
Starting Up and Legalizing Your Tutoring Business

So, you want to be a tutor? You have found your tutoring niche and are ready to start up and legalize your business. Before you can begin, however, it is in your best interest to develop the following: a tutoring philosophy, a vision statement, and a mission statement. After these aspects of your tutoring business have been planned, the next steps are obtaining your business license and a business checking account, figuring out where you will be conducting business, and developing forms for your tutoring business.

Developing a Tutoring Philosophy

When I started tutoring, it was important for me to know why I was tutoring. Most importantly, it was essential for my clients to know why I was in the business of tutoring. At that point, I decided to craft my tutoring philosophy, vision statement, and mission statement. There are three aspects of planning a learning organization, and the first aspect is developing a tutoring philosophy. A tutoring philosophy allows you to practice tutoring according to your tutoring beliefs and knowledge. Oftentimes clients will hire you based upon your views about tutoring (discussed later in chapter 3).

Please take some time to answer these questions to help develop your tutoring philosophy.

1. Why did you decide to become a tutor?

_____
_____
_____
_____
_____

2. What is your definition of tutoring?

_____
_____
_____
_____
_____

3. How do you think children or adults learn best?

_____
_____
_____
_____
_____

4. What is your definition of learning?

_____
_____
_____
_____
_____

5. Do you think all children and adults can learn? Why or why not?

_____
_____
_____
_____
_____

Your answers to these five questions will help you develop your tutoring philosophy and will help with the other critical aspects of planning a successful learning organization—your tutoring business.

Developing Vision and Mission Statements

The second aspect of planning your tutoring business is to develop a vision statement. Constandse (2012) defines a vision statement as "A vivid idealized description of a desired outcome that inspires, energizes, and helps you create a mental picture of your target. It could be a vision of apart of your life, or the outcome of a project or goal," (para. 1). Your vision statement will serve as the foundation of your tutoring business, and it should not be extremely detailed. For example, your vision could simply be the following: "I am offering services to students because I believe that all students can learn with the right teaching ingredients."

The third aspect of planning your tutoring business is to develop a mission statement. MindTools, Ltd. (2010) contends that "A mission statement defines the organization's purpose and primary objectives. Its prime function is internal—to define the key measure or measures of the organization's success," (para. 2). An example of a mission statement for a tutoring business could be as simple as the following: "In five years, my tutoring business will become a global tutoring service that provides the highest quality of professional and timely customer service."

Here are some questions that can help guide you through developing both your vision and mission statement.

1. What is the purpose of your tutoring business?

_____
_____
_____
_____
_____

2. What values does your tutoring business represent?

_____
_____
_____
_____
_____

3. What type of organizational culture do you want to provide for your tutoring business? In other words, what type of working environment do you envision for your tutoring business?

_____
_____
_____
_____

4. What do you want clients to say about your tutoring business?

_____
_____
_____
_____

5. How will you carry out your vision statement and mission statement?

_____
_____
_____
_____

It will probably take some brainstorming to come up with your tutoring philosophy, vision statement, and mission statement. You may find yourself coming back a month later and tweaking both your tutoring philosophy and mission statement. All these aspects of planning your tutoring business will be helpful in the near future for your business and should always be in the forefront of every transaction.

Robbins and Coulter (2007) contend:

Organizations need both a vision and mission statements to align their actions, behaviors, and decisions with the purpose they exist for; this forces managers to identify what it is in business to do, what goals to draft, and what strategies to follow in order to have a sense of direction or else the organization will be chaotic, inefficient, ineffective, and unproductive (p. 210).

All these aspects of planning your tutoring business will help identify who you are as a tutor and what your business stands for. After you are satisfied with your tutoring philosophy and your vision and mission statements, it's time to start considering writing or investing in a business plan.

> **EXPERT'S ADVICE:** Have you ever done business with an individual or company based upon their vision and mission statement? If you answered yes, then you are doing the right thing. Business owners spend a great deal of time communicating their desires regarding their business. This piece of information help clients determine if your company is a good fit for their learning needs. As you already know, the world operates according to their belief system. Thus, it is in your best interest to have them and be candid. Each of these components show that you are willing, ready, and able to serve their diverse learning needs.

The Importance of a Business Plan

How does a business plan relate to your tutoring business? A business plan is like a road map that guides you to the destination of your choice. In other words, it's a formal way of looking at your business and a great document to have, especially if you ever consider expanding your tutoring business.

You may be thinking that you do not need a business plan at the moment. I must admit that I thought the same thing when I first started tutoring. In fact, I told myself that I would test it out, but I quickly realized that teaching was going to stick around in my life for many years to come. It wasn't until three years later that I seriously decided to devote more time to expanding my tutoring business.

> **EXPERT'S ADVICE:** You may wonder why I do not go into a great deal of information right now. This is because the business plan is not the main concern at this point. You have to understand that you are trying this out as a home-based business. However, if you are planning on expanding your tutoring business, then you should definitely check out my *Dr. Alicia Holland's Expanding your Tutoring Business* series.
>
> I do go in-depth about business plans. For now, focus on building a demand for your tutoring practice and improving your skills as an effective tutor.

Obtaining the Business License and Business Checking Account

Congratulations! You have done the hard part—planning your tutoring business. Now, it's time for you to legalize it by getting your business licenses and/or business permit and business checking account. Depending on the state and location of your business, you will need to get a business license. A business license allows you to conduct business using either your name or a business name, and it can be obtained at the county clerk's office. At the clerk's office, you will be required to conduct a search to see if your business name is already in use. Typically, the clerk's office will allow you to use one of its computers to search the online databases of all businesses in the county or state. Business licenses are not expensive and must be obtained if you plan on running a tutoring business.

Determining the Location and Hours of Operation

You are almost ready to open your doors for business. The next aspects of your business you need to determine are the location and hours of operation. Are you currently operating from home or are you already established in an office space or designated area? Wherever you conduct tutoring sessions will impact your hours of operation. Here are a few other factors to think about when setting tutoring hours.

1. What age groups (including adults) are you servicing?

_____

_____

_____

_____

2. Are you willing to conduct sessions either in the student's home or at a designated area?

_____
_____
_____
_____
_____

3. How many hours can you dedicate to starting your tutoring business?

_____
_____
_____
_____
_____

4. Do you work full-time? If so, how will you manage your tutoring business hours?

_____
_____
_____
_____
_____

If you were able to answer these questions, then you should have a better idea of the hours that you will be available to tutor and in which location.

Let's look at a scenario regarding a home-based private tutor.

SCENARIO: "I really love my night job!"

Fiona Paris works with school-age learners. She also has a full-time job, but Fiona gets to leave her job before 4:00 p.m. Given this schedule, Fiona is able to tutor children from 5:00 p.m. to 8:00 p.m., which means she can only serve about three learners per day. In her business plan, Fiona has projected that she would serve at least five students per day during the school week and or weekends. According to Fiona's current work schedule, she is not able to meet those projections.

1. Do you think that Fiona should adjust her business plan to a more realistic goal? Why or why not?

_____
_____
_____
_____
_____

2. Is it the right time for Fiona to cut back on her full-time job? Why or why not?

_____
_____
_____
_____
_____

EXPERT'S ADVICE: This is where her business plan comes into play. Fiona needs to ask herself, "Will I be able to commit myself to my business and meet the goals set forth in my business plan?"

By all means, it's important to analyze your hours of operation to determine whether your tutoring business is moving in the right direction. Are you wondering what hours I tutored each day? For the first two years, I only tutored clients in grades K through eight, since my teaching certifications were in these areas. Most clients needed assistance with both math and reading. After quickly realizing that tutoring was a productive avenue for me, I later devised a plan to accommodate high school, adult, and clients with special needs.

Just recently, I started tutoring high school and college students in math, science, statistics, and education courses. This change has required that I devote more hours to tutoring if I want to keep my clientele and grow my tutoring business. Thus, I am opting to tutor school-aged children exclusively from 4:00 p.m. to 8:00 p.m. and other clients by appointment only. This opens up my schedule for other opportunities (discussed later in chapter 6) that will come in handy when business is slow.

The Tutoring Environment

The tutoring environment is the most important concept to consider when tutoring. There are four components of a tutoring environment.

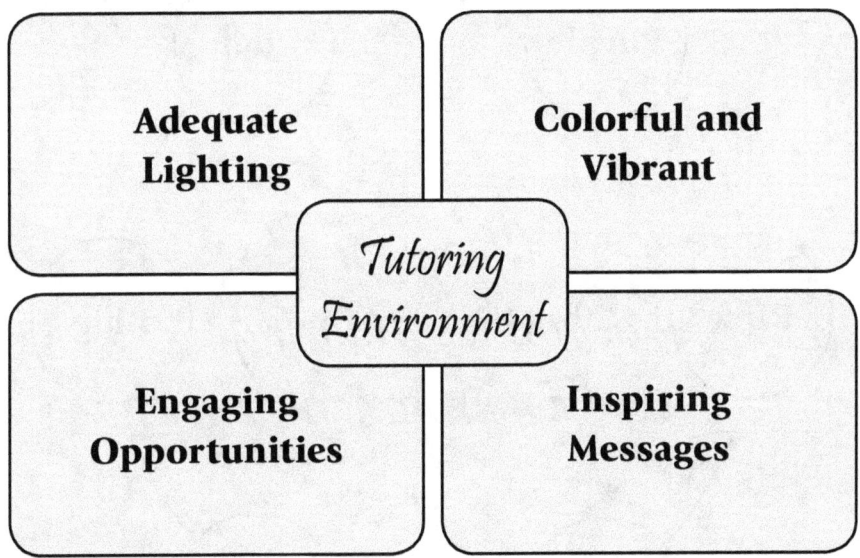

The first component, *Lighting*, is key. Lighting should be medium, and students should be able to see their assignments. Depending on the time of the session, the natural light from the sun brings a sense of freshness and illumination. In my experience, I've noticed that students are more focused when the main lights are turned off and alternative lighting, such as a lamp, is used.

The second component, *Colorful and Vibrant*, is also important. The physical environment should attract positive channels of energy so that clients can concentrate on their needs. Learners tend to do well under certain colors. Did you know that there are some colors that spark the body, mind, and spirit to sync?

The most common colors that should be used in the tutoring environment include the following: (a) Red; (b) Blue; (c) Yellow; (d) Green; (e) Pink; and (f) Purple.

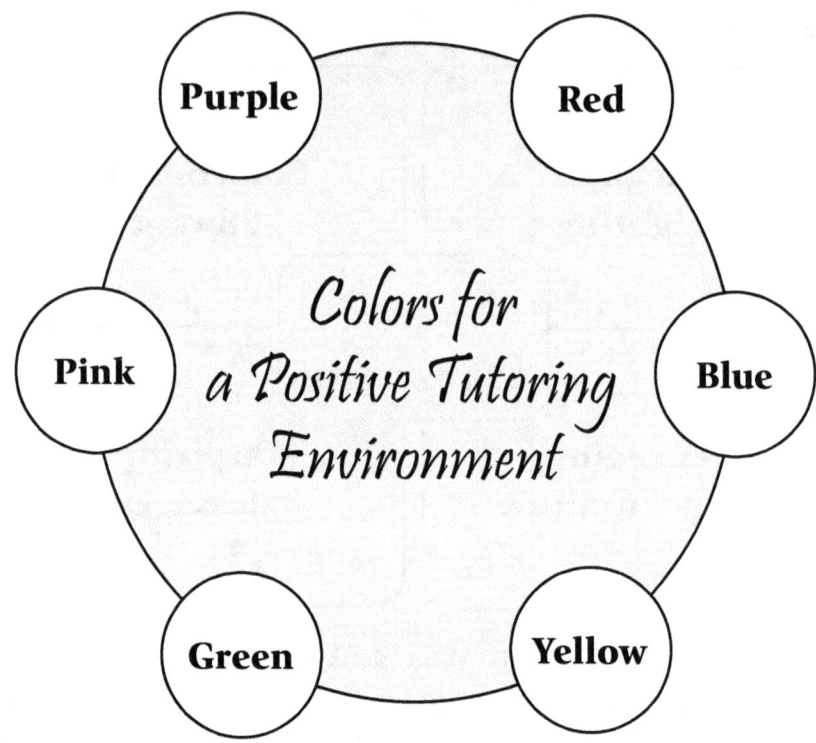

Each of these colors help individuals feel and function a certain way. Therefore, it is very important to ensure that your tutoring environment has a balance so that your clients can reap the benefits.

In terms of the third component, *Engaging Opportunities* should be used to connect with students. Examples of how tutors can get students engaged is by having some sort of visual representation of learning such as an whiteboard, or handheld device (i.e., iPad or tablet). Learners will definitely be engaged with the lesson if they have a chance to show what they know as well. After all, learners do want to be engaged in whatever they are learning so tutors should allow them to do so.

The last component, *Inspiring Messages*, is also part of a healthy tutoring environment. Throughout the environment, inspirational messages will create a positive atmosphere. These inspirational messages should range from Chinese proverbs to everyday words of wisdom. For example, "Believe that the sky is the limit." These are words that can help individuals move toward their life purpose, and it is important to ensure that your clients are hearing positive messages. The reality is that some of your clients may hear such messages at your tutoring practice. Thus, it is very important to never underestimate the power of words, especially motivating and inspiring words.

Let's look at two examples of how to design your physical environment for your tutoring sessions.

Design #1: Tutoring Office

	Inventory/Resource Room	Tutor's Office Space
Tutoring Room #1		
Tutoring Room #2	**Waiting Area/Common Area**	
Tutoring Room #3		
Technology Station		

This design is an ideal tutoring office for a private tutor. There are three tutoring rooms, so you can set up three different clients in each room. Each tutoring room should be equipped to work with either one client or a small group of clients (no more than three). While the tutoring room will not be as large as a typical classroom, it should be large enough to accommodate a small group of students. In addition to tutoring rooms, there should be at least two computer rooms and a testing room to schedule progress-monitoring assessments and pre-assessments. Since you are conducting tutoring sessions for at least one hour at a time, it is important to have a waiting area for parents. This area should be comfortable and welcoming to visitors. Depending on the size, it should include chairs, magazines, info commercials, books, tables, and artwork.

Design #2: Home Office for Private Tutoring

Client Workspace	Client Workspace	Tutor's Desk
Computer Station		Bookcase
		Bookcase

There is not a great deal of space in this design. If you are already using your home office for private tutoring, you may have noticed that there is not a lot of room. It gets the job done, however, until your business expands tremendously (and helps you save on your income taxes). A teacher's desk, a computer station, at least three bookcases, and two workspaces for clients can fit in a standard ten-by-twelve-foot room. It will take imagination to create the environment you would like for tutoring. The bottom line is that it can be done with either one of the aforementioned designs.

> **EXPERT'S ADVICE:** When it comes to selecting a tutoring office for your home-based business, it is always a good idea to start out small, even if it means at your own home. This could look very different because there are additional options such as coffee shops, libraries, your clients' homes, and so forth.
>
> If you are lucky enough to find office space that is reasonable and fits your hours of operation, this would be ideal. However, if you have a small clientele base, then it would make much more sense to use other options to serve your clients.
>
> The bottom line is that either design will work. It just depends on how fast your tutoring practice grows and what you are willing to pay for office space as a home-based tutoring business owner.

Developing Business Forms for Your Tutoring Business

In any business, you will need certain information from clients that will enable you to perform your services; the same is true in the tutoring industry. There are certain forms needed when working with school-aged clients. These forms are the following: (1) tutoring services registration form, (2) tutoring guidelines, (3) authorization for release of information,

(4) Release from Liability Form, and (5) client policies and procedures.

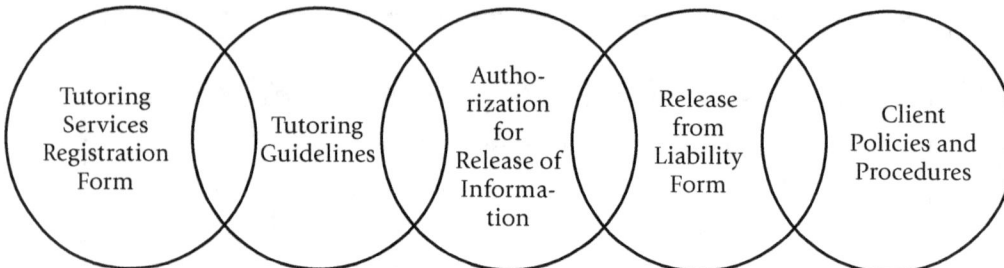

Tutoring Services Registration Form

This form should be given to all clients so that you have contact information on file. This form should also include items that will be helpful to you. For example, you may want to know how they found out about your tutoring services. If the client is school-aged, then you will want to include questions inquiring about the name of his/her current school, grade level, and teacher. This form also affords you the opportunity to inquire about whether clients are interested in future sessions in the summer, fall, or spring.

Tutoring Guidelines

Tutoring guidelines should be written for all parties involved, which include the tutor, the parent, and the client. The guidelines for the tutor should include being on time, being prepared for each lesson, and being professional and ethical at all times. The guidelines for the parents should include providing all enrollment information and paying all tutoring sessions either after services have been rendered or in advance. For the client, it is important to include guidelines that will foster the expected behaviors and expectations in a tutoring session. For example, you want to make sure that clients are aware that they should bring all class-related materials, such as textbooks or important notes, to the sessions. Also, you may want to include that you expect for all clients to complete any assigned tasks and be engaged in the tutoring session.

Authorization to Release Information Form

This form should be used only when a client requests that information be shared with a third party, such as school personnel, enrollment counselor, etc. Typically, at the first session, this form should be filled out so there is no delay in providing information for the client. If you wish, you can save paper and only give the form to clients who request it. This strategy works well, too.

Another example of when to use this form is when a client has another party bring his/her child to tutoring sessions. This will save you from legal battles and serves as a safety precaution for all parties involved.

Release from Liability Form

This form should be used for all clients, especially if you meet with clients outside of your tutoring office. Typically, this form should be signed prior to tutoring sessions. Also, you should be very clear about what tutoring is and the purpose of an adult being present if tutoring sessions are being conducted outside of your tutoring practice.

•••

SCENARIO: "If I Hire You, You Do What I Want"

Preston, a math tutor, who was working with a client with special needs had taken over the position from another tutor. He quickly realized that he was making a difference in the client's life. After six months of tutoring, the parent started leaving the house either 30 minutes into the tutoring session or 10 minutes before the session ended.

Preston could not leave on time because the child would be left unattended. In another incident, the parent ordered Preston to write a letter to the school demanding answers about her child. A year and a half later, Preston made the difficult decision to resign as the tutor of record. The client had made significant progress as he transitioned from middle school to high school. The parent begged him to stay and even offered him more money, but Preston still decided to resign.

1. How do you think Preston handled the situation?

_____
_____
_____
_____
_____

2. How would you have handled the situation?

_____
_____
_____
_____
_____

> **EXPERT'S ADVICE:** Preston was caught in a tough situation. While he was doing his job as the tutor, the parent's actions were very unacceptable. Tutoring is not babysitting; it is a profession. The fact that the parent took advantage of the situation is unbelievable. Prior to servicing clients, you need to explain what is expected of parents while their child is receiving tutoring services and have them sign business forms that pertains to your tutoring practice's way of conducting business.
>
> You can find these forms and additional resources at www.becomingabettertutorblog.com to help with your tutoring business needs.

Client Policies and Procedures

This document is part of the lifeblood of your tutoring business, because it serves as the tutoring contract between you and the clients. In other words, this document could serve as a legally binding contract obligating clients to fulfill financial responsibilities in exchange for the services that you have provided to them.

The language in this document should be written on a readable level (no higher than eighth grade) so that clients understand what they are purchasing and/or agreeing to.

Here are some questions that you should consider when trying to create your tutoring contract.

1. How will you communicate to clients your reason for offering tutoring services?

_____
_____
_____
_____
_____

2. Will you implement a policy for late arrivals or pickups?

_____
_____
_____
_____
_____

3. How will you communicate your session fees to clients?

_____
_____
_____
_____
_____

4. Will you implement a policy to have clients notify you of a cancellation? If so, have you thought about a reasonable time frame?

_____
_____
_____
_____
_____

5. Would you need a policy about allowing food during tutoring sessions?

_____
_____
_____
_____
_____

6. Did you include your complete contact information and tutoring schedule, if applicable?

_____
_____
_____
_____
_____

7. Do you think you will need to include an extra box for additional information (e.g., For Office Use Only)?

_____
_____
_____
_____
_____

Once you have answered these questions, you should be ready to craft your tutoring contract or the form for client policies and procedures. Happy writing!

In this chapter, you learned where to get your business licenses, how to develop your mission and vision statements, and how to create your tutoring forms. You are officially ready to open your doors; but before you do (or if you have already), let's look at how to bring clients to you.

Part II:
Establishing and Promoting Your Tutoring Business

CHAPTER 3:
Effectively Attracting Clients to Your Tutoring Business

How did you find out about your favorite product or service? I'm sure that you saw an ad in a newspaper, online, or even on television. Just like you discovered these individuals or companies, your clients need to find you. If you are reading this chapter, you have made the serious commitment to offer your tutoring services.

Let's look at how to bring clients to your tutoring business. It's important to start thinking about the following questions:

1. How will I market my tutoring business?

_____
_____
_____
_____

2. Will I need a website? Why or why not?

_____
_____
_____
_____
_____

3. Who are my potential clients?

_____
_____
_____
_____
_____

4. How can I seal the deal to offer my tutoring services to them?

_____
_____
_____
_____
_____

Have you answered these questions? If not, it's okay, because we will look at the many ways to advertise your tutoring business. If you have answered all these questions and are already tutoring, then maybe it's time to look at other avenues of attracting customers to your business.

Let's look at two categories of marketing your services in the tutoring industry—basic marketing strategies and advanced marketing strategies.

Basic Marketing Strategies

Basic marketing strategies are strategies that are low cost and easy to use when first starting your tutoring business. Oftentimes you are using these strategies and may not even know it. We will explore a few of the marketing strategies that can be used to attract clients to you. These strategies are the following: (1) online advertising, (2) local advertising, and (3) networking.

Online Advertising

Many jobs are being posted online. In today's society, there are many tutoring sites where you can post your tutoring profile for a nominal fee.

I have used social networking sites, such as Facebook, Twitter, and LinkedIn, as avenues for advertising my services. I also use Craigslist to advertise my services, as Craigslist allows one to post services in numerous categories. In other words, there will only be one copy of the posting visible. Craigslist monitors postings, and if they see that there is a similar or repeated posting, they will delete the message or flag it as spam. Please use your own judgment when both posting and applying for tutoring jobs, as there seem to be scams targeted at tutors. A good rule of thumb is to post only in your area (that's if you conduct your tutoring sessions in your own home or at your client's home) and respond to potential clients who are within your geographic region.

Local Advertising

If you prefer to post locally, then you should seek locations where there's a great deal of traffic. While posting flyers in schools may be a great idea, many public school districts either do not allow flyers about tutoring or have a rigid, tedious process where one may have to wait several months before gaining exposure. For this reason, I recommend posting services in other areas and consider offering your current client an incentive to refer others to your tutoring services. After clients have made a decision to choose my tutoring services, I offer them a referral coupon so that they can refer others to my tutoring business. In exchange, clients are able to get a free or discounted tutoring session. Word of mouth is the best way to advertise. Past or present clients are already aware of how you conduct business as a tutor and have testimonies about their children's successes, so they are a great way to advertise. If you show gratification to your satisfied clients, your business will continue to grow.

Networking

Networking is important in every industry. If you are tutoring locally, then it would make sense to partner or serve as a vendor at a local event to market your services. Oftentimes other small businesses will allow you to advertise in their buildings in exchange for the same exposure and/or services. For example, there was a small business owner who owned a salon and whose daughter needed assistance in math. We informally discussed tutoring in general while I got my hair done. The following day, we held a tutoring consultation and entered into an agreement that for each six sessions she would give me one free hairstyle. This hairstyle ranged from $180.00 upward. After the tutoring consultation, I realized that her daughter only needed six sessions to improve her area of weakness. In this case, both parties were happy. The stylist was able to get the help for her daughter, and I was happy to help her daughter and receive a microbraid hairdo. From a business perspective, each owner demonstrated honesty and commitment and was results-oriented, which resulted in numerous referrals. Please beware that every client will not be willing to enter such an agreement, and tutors should be selective. In any event, networking is a strategy that should be considered, especially if you are a small business owner.

> **EXPERT'S ADVICE:** When you are trying to grow your tutoring practice, it is very important to start out with one of these three basic marketing strategies. That way, you have not spent a great deal of money. Not to mention, if you are doing a great job, then satisfied clients will spread the good news so be prepared for the additional business. You may also find that you will need a website until you are truly ready to expand your tutoring business. At that time, you will definitely need to consider some of the other advanced marketing strategies.

Advanced Marketing Strategies

These are strategies that are used to attract more clients when a business is already established and has a good cash flow. We will explore a few of the marketing strategies that can be used to expand your marketing repertoire. These strategies are the following: (1) offering sponsorships, (2) getting a website started, (3) using direct mailing and newsletters, (4) joining your local Chamber of Commerce, and (5) e-mail advertising.

Offering Sponsorships

Are you into sports? Local youth sport coaches are always looking for business owners or individuals to sponsor them. This includes providing certain things for them, like buying their uniforms and equipment. This type of sponsorship will allow you visibility with your targeted audience if you plan on working with K-12 students.

Another way to advertise your tutoring business is to sponsor other community events, such as a luncheon for an event. Let's say that you belong to a professional organization; you can always sponsor a lunch or set up a booth that displays your tutoring services. You never know who's from your geographical area.

Getting a Website Started

A website will be a good investment because clients are always surfing the Internet and could easily find your services. There are many web-hosting services available to choose from, such as godaddy.com, yahoo.com, google.com, and others. When creating your website, please include the following: (1) a home page with an advertisement about your services, (2) services that you offer, (3) information about the company, and (4) contact page for potential clients.

Home Page	**Services Offered**	**Company Information**

	Contact Page	

Home Page

Your home page should consist of your advertisement and should entice your prospective clients to want to know more about your services. It wouldn't hurt to add a picture or a logo that brands your tutoring business. This is the first place that potential clients will stop, and it should be a positive reflection of your tutoring business.

Services Page

This is where you should explain why clients should choose you as a private tutor. Be sure to list the services that you provide along with any pricing information. For example, my potential clients must e-mail or call for current rates. This allows you to interact directly with them, enabling you to justify your rates. You may also want to include a column titled, "What's New at [Your Tutoring Business]." In this section, you should include any events that have recently occurred or any upcoming events.

Information about [Your Tutoring Business]

This is where you provide the history of your tutoring business and how it got started. Most people are interested in how this service becomes available to others. This would also be a great place to post client testimonials to confirm that you do offer high-quality services to your clients.

Contact Us

On your contact page, it's important to have the phone number, address, and e-mail address of your business. Also, if your web service has the capability, it would be helpful to have a link for clients to find driving directions to your tutoring business. In addition, it would be a great idea to include a customer contact form, which allows potential clients to ask questions about your tutoring services and leave their contact information. This allows you to contact them and answer any questions that they may have about your tutoring services.

Using Direct Mailing and Promotional Products

Direct mailing is a marketing strategy worth trying once your business has grown. You can either choose to mail out your marketing materials or use online direct marketing services. In either case, you would need to create a contact list or purchase a contact list of potential clients who may be interested in your tutoring services. There are various companies you can use to purchase contact information, such as geoselector.com.

Promotional products are definitely a great way to give your tutoring business a jump start. These items could be small, such as mouse pads, pens, pencils, notepads, key chains, and other inexpensive items. Ideally, these items would be given out to first-time clients or prospective clients.

Joining Your Local Chamber of Commerce

Does the area where you are locating your tutoring business have a Chamber of Commerce? If so, you should strongly consider joining it once you have found an office space. The investment that you make with the Chamber of Commerce will definitely go a long way for your business. This organization is dedicated to helping new businesses flourish and will provide a network of resources to help build your tutoring business.

E-mail Advertising

On your website, you should have a newsletter sign-up form so that your visitors will sign up for exclusive tips and so much more. This is your opportunity to market directly to your target audience. Your potential clients trust you enough to give out their contact information, including e-mail. Therefore, you should treat it as a privilege.

When using e-mail advertising, there are a few guidelines that you should follow to ensure that you do not lose your target audience.

Below are five guidelines that you should follow:

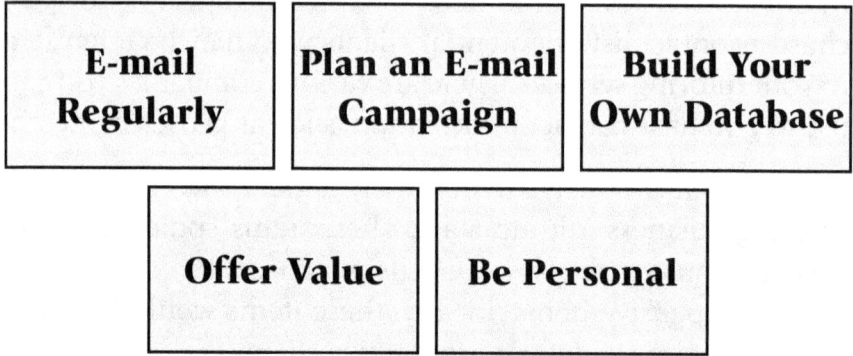

The first guideline, *E-mailing Regularly,* is very important because most individuals read their e-mails every day. However, it does not mean that you should send e-mails to clients every day.

The second guideline, *Plan an E-mail Campaign,* requires that you pre-plan out a few e-mails to send to your targeted audience. For example, you may decide to run a back-to-school special. It would make sense to run a 6-week e-mail campaign with weekly e-mails. These e-mails would be sent, in addition to, the monthly newsletters that your clients would be receiving. The bottom line is that you should not abuse this great opportunity to interact with your clients.

The third guideline, *Build Your Own Database*, requires that you place a newsletter sign-up form on your website. Did you think that your business would grow overnight? I sure hope not! Rather than spend money on an e-mail list, you should try to build your own database first. If your target market is very broad, then it would not hurt to look into purchasing an e-mail list in the future. Also, if your marketing budget permits, then it would not be a bad investment to purchase an e-mail list. When following this route, you just have to weigh your options and plan accordingly.

The fourth guideline, *Offer Value*, requires that you give your target audience something of value to them. Let's face it . . . people signed up because they trust that you would deliver value. Besides seeking their business, you should offer your target market something special. For instance, you could offer them something free and of value to them.

The fifth guideline, *Be Personal*, requires that you keep it real with your targeted audience. Rest assured, they will read between the lines in your e-mails and opt out. Therefore, you always want to be very personal and have their best interests at heart. Please understand that this does not mean that you have to divulge your personal lives to them. Instead, you need to treat them as people and the respect will be there. If your target audience is not in the market for your services, then more than likely, they will refer your tutoring practice to families that are in need of a great tutoring program.

> **Expert's Advice:** At this point, you will need a website for your tutoring practice. Most of your clients will find you online so you should consider spending the most money to ensure that you have an interactive community. As your tutoring practice grows, your outlook about how you can service your clients will grow as well. Thus, the best advice that I can give you is to stay positive and open-minded on how you can attract clients to your tutoring practice.

In this chapter, you have probably realized that it really does not matter which marketing method you use; you should use the strategies that yield the most traffic yet are cost-effective to your tutoring business. The bottom line is to stay within your marketing budget while letting your potential clients know that you offer a variety of services that are tailored to them.

CHAPTER 4:
Pricing to Win: A Choice That Will Make or Break Your Tutoring Business

At this point, you have probably realized that there are many sources of lifeblood for your tutoring business. When it comes to pricing your tutoring business, you will need to understand what your prices cover, research your competition, and apply some pricing strategies to get clients. Each of these tasks is considered a capillary of your tutoring business. In this chapter, you will learn about the capillaries of your tutoring business and learn how to price your services to get clients calling your tutoring practice.

Understanding Your Tutoring Prices

First off, there are several questions that you need to consider when setting tutoring rates.

These questions are the following:

1. Does the cost cover resources used with the client?

2. Will you be traveling to the client or will the client come to you for services?

3. Are you home-based or practicing in an office? If not, do you meet in a free location, such as a local library or coffee shop?

4. What other expenses are you incurring with tutoring?

These are some basic questions that can help guide you in understanding what expenses may need to be paid with tutoring fees. Once you have a good idea about what will be included in tutoring fees, then it's important to research your competition to make sure that you do have the competitive advantage.

Researching Your Tutoring Competition

You must understand that you are not the only person who provides tutoring. There are other individuals or businesses that will be in competition with you. How do you set yourself apart from your competition? Well, we know that most large tutoring companies have access to resources that individuals and small businesses do not always have. So, that is where we have to level the playing field in the tutoring industry. This is where you can begin to minimize the threats and capitalize on the opportunities. For example, large tutoring businesses have websites. This is an arena where you can compete and gain the competitive advantage. Have you noticed that their prices are not disclosed on their websites? The reason businesses do not post their prices is that anyone who knows their web URL is able to look at their website, resulting in a loss for them and dampening their chances of having the competitive advantage. Oftentimes these large tutoring businesses charge $75 per hour or more, which is expensive for the average family.

The best place to look for private tutors' rates is online. Sites like Craigslist and care.com allow tutors to post hourly rates. Your competition is any person who was listed earlier in this book as being qualified to tutor. For example, if you are tutoring high school math, you want to make sure that you have thoroughly researched what other high school tutors are charging for their services and go from there.

SCENARIO:
"An Hour Late and Several Dollars Short"

Bridget, a private tutor with ten years of teaching experience in high school math (all subjects), has just received a phone call about her tutoring services. The potential client wants her to work with her son twice a week for two-hour sessions. Bridget is extremely excited because this is her first client, and she really needs to start making money. Therefore, she immediately takes the job and sets her tutoring fee at $15 per hour.

Thirty minutes later, Bridget gets on the Internet and starts looking for other private high school tutoring rates; she uses Craigslist. Quickly, she realizes that most tutors with her experience charge $35 per hour, and she should have charged the client more.

1. What do you think Bridget should do?

_____

_____

_____

_____

> **EXPERT'S ADVICE:** Can you relate to Bridget? I must admit that I had the same experience when I first started out with my tutoring business. Once you set your tutoring prices with clients, it is not wise to renege on your prices just so that you can benefit. If there is a break in tutoring sessions, however, then it would be more appropriate to ask for the market price. If this happens to you, let it be a lesson, and

> **EXPERT'S ADVICE** *(continued)*
> check current market rates on a regular basis. This time frame can be anywhere from every three to six months or annually—whatever you deem appropriate.

Evaluating Your Potential Clients

You have spent some time researching your competition, but now it is time to "hone in" on the clients. This simply means to track certain information so that you can adequately price your services. Here are some questions to think about:

1. What geographical area are your clients coming from?

_____

_____

_____

_____

2. Based upon your tutoring business location, which neighborhoods or areas are considered low-income, middle-class, and affuent?

_____

_____

_____

_____

This piece of information is only used to make sure your prices are set just right for your clients. As a business owner, however, you need to revisit your mission and vision statements to determine whether your prices those statements.

> **EXPERT'S ADVICE** When I started my tutoring business, I set prices according to the market. This strategy did work for a while until the economy went south. This forced me to rethink the way I set my tutoring prices—and fast. Despite this minor setback, it was still important for me to know which geographical areas I was servicing and what types of clients were attracted to my business. It just made business sense!

Applying Pricing Strategies That Lead to Sales

You may know your worth at this point and what type of clients you are servicing; all this is great news. Have you thought about pricing strategies? There are two pricing strategies that are effective for your tutoring business: (1) tutoring packages and (2) flat-rate tutoring.

Tutoring Packages → ← **Flat-Rate Tutoring**

Tutoring Packages

Tutoring packages are tutoring sessions that are packaged in a certain quantity. For example, tutoring packages can be organized in five-, ten-, fifteen-, or twenty-session groupings. The idea is to get your clients to prepay for sessions up front so that you do not have to worry about collecting payments every session. Typically, the larger the tutoring package, the cheaper the rate. For instance, a client purchases a ten-session tutoring package for $300, while the regular session fee is $35 per hour. This client has saved $50 because he or she has purchased the tutoring package. From a business perspective, this pricing strategy can help with your business cash flow.

SCENARIO: "Can You Supersize It, Please?"

Kara has been running a successful tutoring business, and she is using the tutoring package pricing strategy. Most of her clients have been referrals and already expect to pay in advance. After analyzing her tutoring schedule, Kara realizes that she can service three additional clients. As a result, she posts an ad on Craigslist and gets two immediate responses. Later that day, she holds the tutoring consultations and explains to the parents exactly what their child needs. When it comes to pricing, the parents ask if they can "pay as they go" for the sessions. In other words, they want to pay for each tutoring session after Kara has finished the session. Without giving the parents an option, Kara offers them a tutoring package. The parents reject the offer and explain that they are on a budget and cannot afford to prepay for the sessions. Kara had never experienced clients who opted to pay per session.

1. How do you think Kara should have handled this situation?

___

EXPERT'S ADVICE In Kara's case, she should try to work with the clients, since they may not choose her services because of the price structure. Kara also needs to keep in mind that her competition offers a variety of options for clients to pay for their services. In addition, Kara must remember that potential clients choose private tutors because of the easy terms and reasonable fees.

Flat-Rate Tutoring Fee

A flat-rate tutoring fee is where private tutors set a fee for clients who seek their tutoring services or a fee for traveling to clients to provide their tutoring services. This fee is set, and clients can expect to pay this fee during the duration of the time that they are receiving services. For example, a tutor charges $40 per hour for all tutoring sessions conducted at either his or her home or office space. In the event that the tutor needs to travel to the clients' homes or another location, the tutor can charge an extra $20 for travel expenses that include gas, tolls, or turnpike fees. This will allow tutors to be consistent with their tutoring fees, and clients can know how much they will be paying for tutoring services.

> **EXPERT'S ADVICE** A fresh, new tutoring business should try to attract clients first, but once you have at least three or more clients, it would be wise to look at these pricing strategies. Again, this advice is based upon the assumption that you have analyzed what types of clients are attracted to your business. This information can guide you in providing flexible and affordable pricing strategies for your clients.

In this chapter, you learned how to analyze what your tutoring prices will cover and where to look to research your competition. You also learned the importance of evaluating your potential clients and the difference between two effective pricing strategies.

Part III:
Taking Care of Your Tutoring Business

CHAPTER 5:
Keeping Track of Your Money

At this point, you should be in business, and money is rolling in. Do you really have a plan in place to keep track of your money? If you are reading this chapter, it means that you already have a business checking account. Congratulations! You have taken the first step toward separating your business and personal finances.

Here are a couple of questions to ask yourself.

1. Do I use my business checking account to pay any personal bills? If so, which bills?

_____
_____
_____
_____
_____

2. Why do I use my business checking account when I have a personal checking account to use?

_____

_____

_____

_____

If you answered these two questions, you may have identified bills that are being paid from your business checking account that are really personal expenses. In this chapter, we are going to explore how to make your money work for you.

Establishing Good Credit and Fixing Bad Credit

SCENARIO:
"What You Don't Know Will Hurt You"

Marcus, who had been operating a home-based tutoring business, had decided that he wanted to expand his business. For several months, he searched for office space and found the perfect place (120 feet) to accommodate his needs as a tutor. This office space seemed as if it were heaven sent; all utilities were paid. Marcus only had to worry about making the rent, which was just $350 a month. Marcus was excited because he was tired of watching his clients wait outside or catching them walking around in his kitchen. Besides, he knew that getting an office would bring more clients and build his image as a professional tutor. It seemed as if many opportunities were showering down upon him. Marcus had an opportunity to apply for a *small business loan. He wanted to borrow $5,000 to purchase office furniture and technology, since he offered online tutoring as well.*

Unfortunately, Marcus was denied because of his personal credit; he had some charge-offs and delinquent accounts. Despite the loan denial, the loan specialist was really helpful; she told him that he could reapply after six months. This would allow Marcus to pay of the accounts that were delinquent and fix his bad credit. Marcus felt like he had learned a valuable lesson about starting a home-based business. Nevertheless, he realized that he was taking a gigantic step, which was a good thing for him.

•••

1. If you were in Marcus's situation, how would you have responded to the specialist?

_____
_____
_____
_____
_____

2. What advice would you give to Marcus regarding his personal credit and purchasing items for his tutoring business?

_____
_____
_____
_____
_____

Expert's Advice: In Marcus's case, he thought that since he did not have any business liabilities, he would get the loan. He later learned that his personal credit had to support his claim for his business when he was trying to get a loan. For private tutors, separating your business and personal finances can be a challenge, especially if you are supplementing your income. As a general rule, it is necessary to do, but oftentimes it is not done.

I must forewarn you that if you are interested in becoming a supplemental education service (SES) provider for your state, you must have your finances in order. As I was expanding my own tutoring business, I learned to have business collateral that I could use when it came to borrowing money from a loan company. Business collateral could be real estate, business vehicles, office furniture, and technology. For example, Jason could have used the items for which he had requested the loan as business collateral. In any event, it helps to have some business assets, as they will only help you grow your tutoring business.

In terms of business, good credit would mean paying for a business loan, a vehicle, or rent. This type of credit will only help your tutoring business grow. It wouldn't be a bad idea to get a business credit card, which could help you with many expenses for your business. Most important, please make sure that your personal credit is at least fair, with no delinquent accounts or charge-offs. Your credit report can either help or harm you in expanding your tutoring business. The ability to

> **EXPERT'S ADVICE** *(continued)*
> rent office space can also be affected by having bad credit. The bottom line is to eliminate bad credit and find ways to establish good credit. This decision alone can bring much satisfaction and help expand your tutoring business.

Understanding Cash Flow

Cash flow is the main artery of your business; it keeps everything moving.

You may be wondering exactly what cash flow is. According to the Business Dictionary (2010), "Cash flow is the incoming and outcoming of cash," (para. 1). In other words, it is the payments that you receive from customers. A strategy that could be used to predict a steady cash flow is the use of your tutoring schedule or monthly calendar. Another way to keep track of cash flow is to invest in an accounting software such as Quickbooks or PeachTree.

Using Your Tutoring Schedule

Do you have a tutoring schedule or monthly calendar that you use for booking tutoring sessions? If you do, then you can use it as a tool to help predict your weekly tutoring cash flow. For example, let's say that you have tutoring sessions on Mondays, Tuesdays, and Wednesdays in June. On the first Monday of June, you have five sessions, and each client pays $35 per session. Your cash flow would be $175. On the first Tuesday of June, you only had two sessions, totaling $70, while on the first Wednesday you had three sessions, totaling $105. The cash flow for this week would be $350. If the same tutoring pattern occurs for the rest of the month, then it would be safe to say that for the month of June your projected cash flow would be $1,400.

If you are making at least $500 a month, you are doing well. Depending on your motives and desires for your tutoring business, you might want to start saving most of your tutoring income in order to expand. Again, this depends on your desires for your tutoring business.

Deciding on an Accounting System

Once you start making a lot of money weekly and accepting various forms of payment (money orders, cash, checks, or credit cards), it will be a lot easier to keep track of your cash flow. Purchasing an accounting system is a huge step and investment for your business. As with any other investment, you should always check around for the best price for loaded features. One strategy is to try free trials. QuickBooks and other accounting systems have a free version, which has limited capabilities. It will allow you, however, to make an informed decision on which accounting system to buy. Mainly, you should look for an accounting system that has the capability to predict cash flow, keep an accrual balance, receive and make payments, and create a detailed payment history for each client. This allows you to see which clients are paying the most or least, as this information comes in handy if needed for tax purposes. The bottom line is that you need an accounting system that will make your job easier and keep track of your money.

Basic Bookkeeping for Your Tutoring Business

Have you ever purchased something and tried to return the item without a receipt? How did you feel when the customer service manager rejected your return? Whatever this feeling was, it is the same feeling that will be felt if you do not keep records of business activity, especially if the Internal Revenue Service (IRS) conducts an audit regarding your home-based tutoring business. Not to mention, you want to get in the habit of keeping good business records if you plan on working with the government in the future. Most government contracts will require awarded applicants to have solid financial records so that project expenses can be accounted. In other words, financial audits can be warranted anytime throughout the contract term.

Below are five types of basic records that will need to be kept for your tutoring business:

Revenues and Expenses	Cash Expenditures	Inventory Records

Accounts Payable	Accounts Receivable

The first type of records, *Revenues and Expenses*, should be documented each month. Basically, this is a way to show how cash is flowing and leaving the business. For example, individuals can record each transaction that occurs whether it is invoicing clients or receiving payments. If you have hired an accountant, then you will submit this information monthly or on a mutually agreed schedule.

The second type of records, *Cash Expenditures*, is very important. There will be times in which you will make small purchases for the business. This is completely fine as long as you hold on to that receipt. Just to be on the safe side, please try your best to keep these type of expenses to a minimum.

The third type of records, *Inventory Records*, should be kept on file. You may be wondering how this applies to your tutoring business. If you have any office supplies, instructional supplies, or products, you will need to keep up with the inventory. In some states, there is a sales and use tax that must be paid on these items. Mainly, it is products such as workbooks, books, and so forth.

The fourth and fifth types of records, *Accounts Payable and Accounts Receivable*, are important in understanding how your tutoring business is performing. These records will need to be used with any business deals, such as applying for a line of credit or expanding to other revenue streams. These records are also called profit-and-loss statements that show all cash flow for each given month.

> **EXPERT'S ADVICE:** For the first three years, I was able to use Microsoft Accounting for free until it was discontinued in 2010. This program saved a lot of time for me and was very helpful at tax time and when I wanted to track my business every quarter. At the start of the new year, I will be switching to another accounting system—probably QuickBooks Online. By using QuickBooks Online, I will be able to access my financials "on the go," and I like the other features it offers. I am not advocating one accounting system over the other. You must analyze your own business needs.
>
> I also want to encourage you to take local business classes on how the accounting system of your choice works. You do not want to find yourself running a business that you do not know anything about when it comes to the financial aspect of your business.

The key to keeping track of your money is to understand how the cash flow works in your tutoring business and find a good yet affordable accounting system that will help keep your business running smoothly. You should also be establishing good lines of credit and fixing your bad credit if you have any.

CHAPTER 6:
Staying on Top When Business Is Down

Business is not what it used to be—the uncertainty of the economy and other factors may cause entrepreneurs to rethink their relationships with their clients. This does not necessarily mean that the relationship is going south, but as with any relationship, one wants to make sure that he or she is giving at least 100 percent (or more) effort to ensure that each experience is great, especially for clients. In this chapter, we will explore ways to maintain a good relationship with clients, find ways to cut expenses, and offer special promotions to help keep your tutoring business running.

Maintaining a Good Relationship with Clients

As with any job or career you undertake, you must maintain relationships to be successful in the tutoring industry. This starts with building relationships with your clients. Your clients already know your tutoring style and can be huge influences on new clients. Therefore, you should spend your time and energy making sure that all your clients have positive experiences. Strategies that have been successful in helping maintain tutoring relationships include: (1) following up with clients on a regular basis and (2) sending postcards.

Following Up with Clients Regularly	**Sending Postcards**

Following Up With Clients Regularly

In tutoring, follow-up is critical because your clients will come to you for only a short period of time (if it's a high school or college student or a test- taker). With these clients, you will need to follow up with them to see if they have passed their test(s) or class(es). A simple call or e-mail like the following would work:

Hello [Client's Name],

This is [Your Name], the tutor who helped you with college algebra. Did you pass your test? I hope that you did well, and I look forward to hearing from you. If you need further assistance, please know that I am available and thanks for choosing my tutoring services.

[Your Name]

Another time you should follow up with clients is when they have finished a tutoring program. It is always a good practice to wait at least two weeks to see whether the client was able to successfully transfer the skills and knowledge that were acquired during their tutoring sessions. Once you have followed up with them, you should plan to follow up with them again in about two months and finally at the end of the term.

You may think of other ways of following up with clients, but these are some methods that have proven effective in either getting referrals from clients or in the clients or their family members becoming repeat customers.

Sending Postcards

Sending postcards is preferable to sending e-mail these days. For instance, for special occasions like birthdays or holidays you could send postcards to your clientele. Clients enjoy receiving postcards that praise them or wish them a happy birthday. This makes them feel special, and it should be done only on special occasions.

• •

SCENARIO: "You Did Remember!"

Cassidy, a twelve-year-old, had an upcoming birthday at the end of the month. Her tutor, Jackie, never said anything about her birthday during tutoring sessions because the time was always dedicated either to homework or working on a new skill. Two days before her birthday, Cassidy received a birthday wish in the mail from her tutor, and was she proud!

Ever since Cassidy received the postcard, she has been extremely eager to attend her tutoring sessions.

• •

1. How do you remember your clients' birthdays?

_____
_____
_____
_____

2. What are additional strategies to use postcards in your tutoring practice?

_____

_____

_____

_____

Handling Conflicts and Nonpayment

If you have crafted your client policies and procedures strategically and clearly, you should not have many conflicts. As you know, however, you will probably experience at least one conflict, and you need to know how to handle it.

Robbins and DeCenzo (2007, p. 349) present five questions that can help you determine whether a situation might justify conflict.

These five questions are the following:

1. Are clients [parents and adult clients] afraid to admit ignorance and uncertainties to you?
2. Do you concentrate so hard on reaching a compromise that you lose sight of key values, long-term objectives, or the organization's welfare?
3. Do you believe that it is in your best interest to maintain the impression of peace and cooperation in your unit, regardless of the price?
4. Is there an excessive concern in your tutoring business not to hurt the feelings of others?
5. Is there a lack of new ideas?

These five questions will help you determine whether conflict is present or approaching and whether it is constructive to improve services or business practices. As a business owner, these five questions can guide you in making the right decisions, with the best interests of both your clients and your business in mind.

Another form of conflict is nonpayment, which can present a problem. I have learned how to take a deposit on future sessions and to obtain payment prior to services being rendered, which has helped with the clients who are slow in paying. This strategy forces them to pay for your services in advance but also gives them the benefit of not purchasing a tutoring package. If you implement a policy where services must be paid for prior to instruction, then nonpayment will not be an issue for you. These are some of the real-world conflicts that you may experience in the tutoring industry.

Finding Ways to Cut Expenses

We are living in a society where saving the Earth and going green is non-negotiable for some and optional for others. For your tutoring business, there are ways that you can cut expenses and save both the Earth and money. Some strategies include: (1) e-mailing, (2) printing only what you need, and (3) recycling office supplies.

E-mailing

For a variety of reasons, e-mail has always been my preferred way to communicate, and most of my clients enjoy e-mail as well. Using e-mail allows you to communicate, and all communication is recorded and saved for future reference. From the onset of our tutoring relationship, I tell clients that all communication will be electronic. Clients have the option, however, to receive paper copies of all communication, as well as invoicing, monitoring notes, instructional plans, and other pertinent information.

Printing Only What You Need

We are all guilty of printing documents that do not necessarily need to be printed. Now that you have your own business, printing becomes a major concern, as you are the responsible party for purchasing office supplies.

SCENARIO: "Don't Save the Rainforest. Save Your Paper and Money."

Calix, a language arts and history tutor, used to provide both paper and electronic copies of documents to clients until the economic downturn. In his monthly newsletter, he announced that there would be a lot of changes that would continue to move the organization forward—and saving paper was one of them. He asked clients to indicate their preferred method of communication, and most of them opted for e-mail, while a select few wanted paper communication. After two months, Calix began to see more money in the business checking account; he had saved over $500 by switching communication to e-mail and offering paper mail to the handful of clients who requested paper communication. Can you imagine the smile on Calix's face?

1. How do you save money for your tutoring business?

_____

_____

_____

_____

2. What are some additional strategies that Calix can employ at his tutoring practice to save resources?

_____
_____
_____
_____

Recycling Office Supplies

When we think of recycling, we think about recycling plastic, aluminum, and paper. Did you know that you can take recycling to the next level? With your tutoring business, you can recycle office supplies. For example, old mail can become your new notepad for taking notes when clients call to inquire about your services. There are other uses for old mail, but this one is the most common. In addition, you can always buy recycled office supplies, but do you really want to cut into your budget? The bottom line with recycling office supplies is to plan in advance how to use them and be open to repurposing how an item is used in your office.

Here are some questions that you should consider if you are interested in recycling office supplies:

1. Which items do you not need for their original purpose?

_____
_____
_____
_____

2. How do you plan on using the item(s) again?

_____
_____
_____
_____

These two questions will help steer you in the right direction of recycling your office supplies.

> **EXPERT'S ADVICE:** The reality is that there will be tutors who opt to use the paper route or use a combination of both methods, which is fine. I must admit that I used a lot of paper at the beginning of my tutoring career until I realized that there was a need to have some items in electronic form. In addition, my tutoring business started to expand quickly, and I could not keep up with writing and retyping monitoring notes and instructional plans. In other words, using the paper method worked when my clientele was small. It was not until more clients enrolled that I had to weigh my options of being efficient, accurate, and sane. Now, I use a combination of the two methods; there are some forms that need to be in paper form, while others can be in either format. The bottom line is that you will need to figure out how you can implement technology to help manage the daily operations of your tutoring business.

Offering Special Promotions

Have you ever bought something or recommended a product or service?

Was this simply because you liked the product or service and they (the business) provided something free or at a discount? This concept can be applied to the tutoring world and should be. There are two ways to implement this strategy in your tutoring business: (1) client referral system and (2) discounts.

Client Referral System

As aforementioned, people say that word of mouth is the best way to attract clients. A client referral system should be realistic and enticing for clients to be motivated to use it. For example, free tutoring sessions would a logical reward to clients. Free sessions could be earned in a certain time frame— for example, after the referred client completes ten tutoring sessions, the client who referred him or her will receive a free session, being required to redeem it within sixty days.

Another option is to offer discounts to clients who refer new clients. These can come in the form of discounts of services or products. For instance, you could offer a 10 percent discount of five tutoring sessions for every new client who is referred to you. This is just another strategy to keep your business running smoothly and continue to earn your clients' trust and respect.

In any case, if you are planning on implementing any of these strategies, please make sure that you announce them to your clients. These strategies should be implemented during a common organizational change period for businesses; ideally, you should make organizational changes during the summer months and execute them during the academic calendar year.

> **EXPERT'S ADVICE:** If you are thinking about implementing a referral system, you should try something simple so that you can see how it works. I started a referral system a year after I opened my business. Because there was not much literature on such techniques, I had to learn by trial and error. Please understand that clients do take the referral system seriously, and you should put a lot of thought into it.
>
> Each of these methods is considered a strategy that helps with client retention and aids with building your brand. As a general message, you should always follow up with your clients at least once or twice a month to keep your business in the back of their minds.
>
> Just think about it this way: If you are already providing excellent service, then the clients will automatically come. You want to let current clients know, however, that you do appreciate them and you can continue to show gratitude by offering state-of-the-art tutoring services—and by giving them more reasons to choose you for their educational needs.

Finding Opportunities to Supplement Your Tutoring Income

You may have realized that you need some additional income to cover other business expenses or some personal expenses. Depending on your background and experience in education, there are a myriad of opportunities waiting for you to supplement your tutoring income. Some of the opportunities that we will explore are: (1) substitute teaching, (2) freelance writing, (3) writing grants and business plan proposals, (4) teaching and tutoring online, and (5) working a second job.

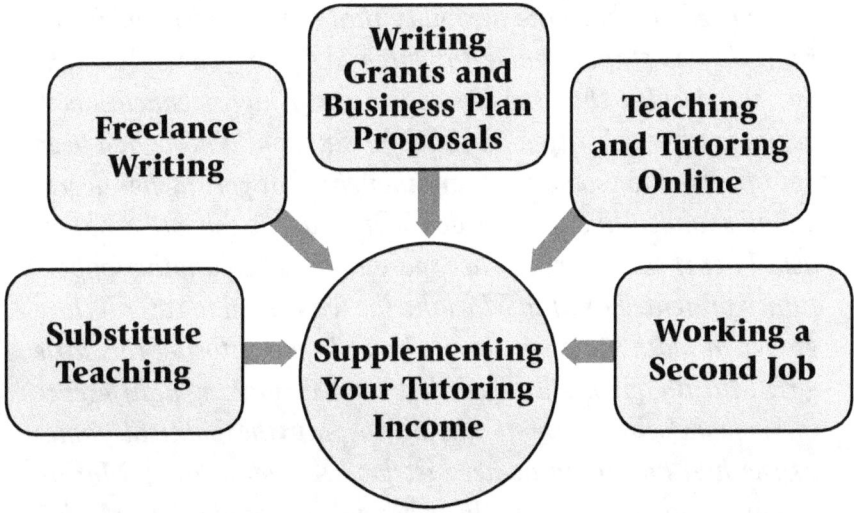

Substitute Teaching

The first opportunity is substitute teaching. As a substitute teacher you take over the class for either a public or private school teacher and are compensated for your services. Substitute teaching is common at the K-12 level and at the college level there are also some substituting opportunities, especially in English as a second language (ESL) classes. Depending on the state in which individuals reside, you may be able to substitute teach as long as they have at least a high school diploma. If individuals have completed a higher level of education, then they will be paid more money to substitute teach. Again, this information depends on each individual school system or state.

SCENARIO: "A Newfound Love"

Mariah, a former math teacher, decided that she would go back into the classroom as a substitute teacher after being out of the classroom for a year. This would allow her to teach when there was a need and have the flexibility that she was seeking. While Mariah was staying home to watch her four-year-old daughter, she decided that she wanted to get a higher education in business after substitute teaching for six months. She had been out of school for some time and thought that getting her degree online sounded like a good idea. One day at school, a parent asked her if she tutored in her spare time. Then another opportunity presented itself to Mariah: she was asked to tutor a third grader in math. She was excited and began tutoring this little girl. Mariah quickly learned that she was making a difference in someone's life without having to play the political game, as she had had to do at her last job. A month later, Mariah received another client—a little boy in fifth grade. So, Mariah was drawing income from substitute teaching and tutoring. Most importantly, she was able to further her education so that more opportunities could come along, and she found the balance between taking care of her family and contributing to the family household.

1. Do you think that Mariah's career path as a tutor will help her with her personal situation? Why or why not?

_____
_____
_____
_____
_____

2. What type of advice would you seek from Mariah who made the bold decision to leave her job to care for her family?

_____
_____
_____
_____
_____

Freelance Writing

The second opportunity is freelance writing. If you have writing skills and are confident about writing for others, you should strongly consider freelance writing opportunities, which include article writing, technical writing, curriculum or content writing, grant writing, and writing business proposals. Each type of writing has different guidelines, and some require a greater time commitment than others. They all have perks and will supplement your income.

Let's look at each type of writing.

Types of Writing

Article Writing	Freelance Writing	Technical Writing	Curriculum or Content Writing

Article Writing

If you choose to write articles for a company, such as textbroker.com, your time spent on an article really depends upon the length of the article. Most articles are between one hundred and eight thousand words, and you will be paid 1¢ a word. You have probably concluded that shorter articles pay less, while longer articles pay more. In a sense this is true, but it also depends on the quality of your writing. In the freelance world, writing pieces are graded on a scale of one to five, with five being the level of a professional writer. If you have the spare time (and money) to work on your writing skills, this is a great opportunity (and investment) that will open more doors for you in the freelance world of writing so that you can supplement your tutoring income.

Technical Writing

Technical writing often pays more, starting at $200 or more per project.

For example, suppose you are contracted to write workplace guidelines or employee handbooks for a particular company—a project lasting only three weeks. The company has agreed to pay you for at least ten hours a week, which means you can expect to be paid at least $900. Of course, this solely depends on the company's budget. Other technical writing projects could involve developing manuals or handbooks or other written materials that require individuals to follow directions. Depending on your knowledge and experience, technical writing can be a lucrative avenue for you.

Curriculum or Content Writing

Curriculum writing is just like technical writing, and it can pay well, depending on whom you are writing for. This type of writing requires curriculum writers to have strong content knowledge and writing capabilities, as projects may require one to develop courses, lessons, and activities.

If you have curriculum development experience and enjoy sharing your knowledge, then you should consider curriculum (or technical) writing.

SCENARIO: "The Unexpected Change"

Tiffany, a mechanical engineer, loved her full-time job but had to leave it suddenly because her husband found a new job in a different state. Tiffany was searching for more jobs on the Internet and came across an ad for a high school tutor in organic chemistry and calculus. She charged these clients $30 per hour and saw them twice a week. The client referred several more *high school students, and she later had over five clients whom she was seeing twice a week. Tiffany only had to work a couple of hours a day to make a decent paycheck that could cover the rent payment and both vehicle payments. She was enjoying her newfound talent—tutoring—and decided that she would also offer her services to college students. It was not long before Tiffany reached an income that almost matched her previous salary. After several months, she learned that she should look for another opportunity to cover the slow months in tutoring. That opportunity happened to be technical writing for a Fortune 500 company—another skill that she possessed.*

1. How do you think that you can supplement your tutoring income?

_____
_____
_____
_____
_____

2. Do you think that Tiffany should work with elementary or middle school students? Why or why not?

_____
_____
_____
_____
_____

Writing Grants and Business Plan Proposals

Writing grants and business plan proposals is lucrative and requires a great deal of time. This type of formal writing also requires that individuals have experience in business and background knowledge about the client's organization. If this information is not provided by the client, then the grant or business plan writer must do the research to support the claims made. Again, depending on the organization, you could land a grant or business plan proposal project starting at $500 or more. The more experience you have in this area and the more evidence you can provide of successfully securing funding, the greater your chances of getting projects. You just have to look for opportunities.

Teaching and Tutoring Online

Did you know that you can teach or tutor online? Yes, you can. Tutoring online allows you to work with clients all over the world. You have two options: (1) work for yourself or (2) work for another tutoring company.

If you are just starting out in the tutoring industry, there are reputable online tutoring companies, such as tutor.com, for which you can work while you build your tutoring business. In terms of teaching online, this could be a virtual K-12 position at a virtual campus. Most of these schools require that online teachers have at least a bachelor's degree or higher. Online teaching presents a lot of opportunities that should be explored if you already have a degree or are working toward one.

> **EXPERT'S ADVICE:** Before you start your tutoring business, it may be a good idea to build your content knowledge in the subjects that you tutor. For example, when I was working as a fifth-grade teacher, I would tutor students from all over the United States in middle school math and science. For my face-to-face tutoring sessions, I would work with both middle and high school students to keep my content knowledge strong. There's an old saying: "If you don't use it, you lose it." The same concept applies to tutoring, so it is extremely important to stay current with your tutoring subjects.

It's in your best interest to use your many talents and to work toward a higher education. The more degrees or experience you have, the more opportunities will be standing at your "career door," which can help you supplement your tutoring business.

In this chapter, you had an opportunity to learn about the importance of keeping in contact with clients and building those relationships. In addition, you learned how to handle nonpayment and strategies to provide incentives to keep clients engaged with your tutoring business. Last but not least, you were presented with additional opportunities to supplement your income when business may be slow during non-peak tutoring seasons.

Part IV:
Data-Driven Strategies for Tutoring

CHAPTER 7:
Tutoring Consultations and How to Handle Them

In today's economy, parents are looking for tutors who are affordable yet qualified and who have great interpersonal skills, especially with younger students. Tutors who are both organized and versatile are sought out in the tutoring profession. Oftentimes parents opt to find college students to tutor their children for three reasons: (1) recent content knowledge, (2) good rapport, and (3) affordable pricing for services. While these are good reasons to choose college students, there is a difference between hiring college students and individuals with tutoring experience. These types of tutors may or may not know how to use strategies that will help tailor lessons to meet clients' specific needs.

Gordon (2009) asserts that highly trained tutors have consistently produced better tutoring results. In general, tutors are effective because they give students more personalized attention. However, over time this effect tends to fade and students resume their earlier learning habits. This is why the tutor's professional education, degrees, special credentials, prior professional experience, and specialized training as a tutor can make a major difference in ensuring that a student achieves better long-term learning gains (para. 13). Parents are looking for individuals who have a background or experience in tutoring.

One of my clients named Michelle shared with me the following:

"I look for tutors who are dependable, knowledgeable, and friendly. It does not matter about the education, as long as they can do the job and help my children. If I had a choice between a college student and a tutor with credentials, I would choose the tutor with credentials if my budget allowed. I like to look at is as 'you get what you pay for.'"

Based upon what Michelle said, it's in the tutor's best interests to have both a reasonable tutoring fee and some professional training as a tutor or some teaching credentials to qualify for most tutoring jobs, especially in the private tutoring sector.

Who Are Your Best Clients?

It's a no-brainer—your best clients are the ones who pay, whether on time or in advance. In fact, there's more to the equation of finding the best client. For example, you need to be emotionally intelligent when dealing with clients, since you may be able to detect needs other than educational, such as financial issues. Believe it or not, these issues affect you indirectly, and you should be more cognizant of how you handle your tutoring consultations.

••

SCENARIO: "Didn't See It Coming"

Karla, a private tutor in elementary math, was hired to work with a fifth grader. At the time she was hired, Karla was used to having all her clients pay in advance. With this particular client, although both parents were working, she had to wait until *the first and the fifteenth to get paid. Karla knew this before she took on the job. The clients were paying on time until the little girl's father lost his job. The fifth grader had a very important test to take within the next two weeks. At this point, Karla had to make a decision about continuing to offer the little girl help in math. Her decision was to continue helping the little girl because she really needed it, and it was the right thing to do. A month passed, and Karla still did not receive any payments from the parents. Karla had invested her time with the little girl and still believed that it was the right decision. Unexpectedly, the client sent a money order in the mail for all the tutoring sessions, along with a $100 bonus. (The little girl's father had found a better-paying job.) Several days later, Karla received four new clients who were referred by these parents. Imagine that!*

1. Do you think that Karla made the right decision? Why or why not?

_____
_____
_____
_____

2. If you could ask Karla any questions about this specific tutoring assignment, what would be those questions?

_____
_____
_____
_____

> **EXPERT'S ADVICE:** In this case, the tutor made the right decision—morally. Karla did what any good-hearted person would have done. As a result, she will forever have had a permanent impact on this family. The fact that Karla received four new clients because of her moral act is a testimony in itself (and shows that she made a good investment).

Mastering Tutoring Interviews and Tutoring Consultations

Tutoring Interviews

In today's society, online advertising is prominent, especially at sites like Craigslist and care.com. This means that online advertising makes it easy for parents to learn about many teachers. Because they want to make the right decision in hiring a private tutor to meet their family's educational needs, parents often opt to conduct interviews. For my first interview as a tutor, I did not know what to expect. After I responded to the Craigslist's posting, I received an e-mail request for an interview within a couple of hours. I did not have time to prepare fully, but I did review the posting.

The parent sent an e-mail request similar to the following:

Hi *(Name)*,

We are looking for a tutor for our two children in math and Spanish. To better assist us in our search, we are conducting initial interviews on Friday. What time are you available?

Thanks!

If you receive an e-mail like this one, it is important to respond immediately and try to get the earliest time available to make a first impression as a quality tutor. If you are deciding what to wear, here's a little advice. Your attire should always be professional—something that you would wear for a business interview.

What to Take with You

Initially, I was not going to bring anything, but an inner voice reminded me that I needed to be prepared. As a result, I gathered all my new- client forms and information. This included the following: (1) tutoring registration form, (2) release of information form, (3) client policies and procedures, (4) sample monitoring notes, (5) release of liability form, (6) tutoring time card, (7) tutoring guidelines, and (8) tentative session dates. (Examples are located in the appendices.)

The day of the interview, a tall, slender woman with brown hair and blue eyes greeted me and walked me to a conference room. As I entered the conference room, I realized that there was only one piece of paper on the table, and I glanced at it to see if I could find my name. Once this woman sat down, she asked many questions.

Using my résumé, she asked several questions.

1. What is your plan to work with students long-term?

2. How would a typical session flow?

3. Do you have any experience teaching Spanish?

After answering these questions, I made a mental note to revamp my résumé in the near future for tutoring positions. The good news about having an extensive résumé is that it helped me qualify for the initial interview. The fact that I brought the new client forms and information demonstrated that I was organized. The interviewer did mention that she could tell that I was prepared and had a good working knowledge of how tutoring should be conducted. Also, I mentioned how tutoring should be a way to help students improve their skills in addition to reinforcing grade- level expectations. Unexpectedly, the interviewer ended the interview and informed me that I would hear from her soon about a follow-up interview. Within twenty minutes, there was an e-mail waiting in my inbox from the interviewer requesting a second interview.

The main theme is being organized and well-versed in your tutoring services. You should also practice conveying why you got into the tutoring business in the first place.

Tutoring Consultations

During the tutoring consultation, much effort goes into collecting rich data about each client's unique needs. Therefore, you may opt to charge new clients a regular tutoring session fee or to waive the consultation fee if the client purchases a tutoring package. While I am not focusing on the business side of tutoring, I must admit that charging consultation fees is a reflection of the tutor being professional and qualified for the tutoring position. The consultation fee can be used to purchase resources that will be used for tutoring sessions. For example, let's say that you have five potential clients who pay a consultation fee of $45—a total of $225. Can you imagine the teaching resources that can be purchased with those consultation fees?

Tutoring consultations should last forty-five minutes to an hour, since parents are paying for them. Generally speaking, the information needed from parents and any other paperwork should be taken care of during that time. Keep in mind that a tutoring consultation may determine whether a client chooses your services. Therefore, it is imperative that you are efficient, organized, attentive, and accurate during a consultation.

Let's check out some scenarios that can help you gain insight into why it is important to be well versed and confident about your tutoring services.

SCENARIO #1:
"You're Too Expensive for My Child"

Linda, a math and reading tutor, had a tutoring consultation scheduled for 3 p.m. Central Standard Time (CST) at her potential client's home. Prior to scheduling the consultation, the parents were aware of the tutoring fee of $35 per hour, which included detailed monitoring notes and assessments. During the consultation, everything went smoothly until it came time to seal the deal. To Linda's surprise, the parents said that they opted to go with a high school student for $15 per hour and wanted Linda to match this price.

Linda declined the offer and thanked them for their interest. However, they still paid for the consultation, which was $35— the same price as a one hour tutoring session.

1. If you were in Linda's situation, how what would you have done?

_____
_____
_____
_____

2. Do you think that Linda made the right decision? Why or why not?

_____
_____
_____
_____
_____

> **EXPERT'S ADVICE:** Wow! I did not think that the tutoring consultation would have turned out this way. This caught me by surprise, too. The reality is that parents have that option and tend to change their minds at the last minute. This is completely fine because you should not want to tutor someone who does not want to be serviced by you. Given this reality, it is very important to have some type of monetary protection because you are in business, and time is money. A good business practice is to charge for tutoring consultations. That way, you will only get serious potential clients. and you will be compensated for your time if parents or adult learners decide to back out of receiving your tutoring services.
>
> Last but not least, you should not lower your worth to gain a client. In this situation, Linda made the right decision by keeping her price because she provided tutoring services and additional perks to show that she is a quality tutor. As long as your tutoring prices are at market, then your focus should be on protecting your brand and working with clients who appreciate both your worth and added value as a professional tutor.

SCENARIO #2:
"Too Many Questions in One Hour"

Christopher, a sought-out tutor in all subjects, was involved in a tutoring consultation with a potential client regarding her seventh-grade son. He had determined that he was able to assist the learner, and the client offered him the position. After accepting the tutoring position, the client wanted to ask all sorts of questions that were borderline inappropriate. For xample, she asked how Chris felt about the surrounding school districts and her child's teacher. The client specifically stated, "How does my child's teacher measure up as a teacher?" Rather than cause a scene, Chris politely told them that he had another appointment and reiterated that he looked forward to working with their child.

1. Do you think that Chris was obligated to answer those borderline questions? Why or why not?

_____
_____
_____
_____
_____

2. How would you have handled the situation?

_____
_____
_____
_____
_____

EXPERT'S ADVICE: I think that Chris handled the situation as best he could. I am assuming that the conversation was about school districts in the community. If it was, it is a very good practice to speak positively at all times. The reality is that you will have clients from many surrounding districts, including private schools and public charter schools. As a result, keep everything related to tutoring and always focus on how you can improve your clients' lives by addressing their diverse learning needs.

I will share with you a lesson that I have learned about tutoring consultations. Even before the recession, clients were hiring tutors strategically. In particular, some clients opted to schedule an interview or a tutoring consultation. When it is your first business and potential clients are interested in your services, a good rule of thumb is to schedule a tutoring consultation rather than an interview. A tutoring consultation allows you to showcase your qualities as a tutor and make personal connections with the client and/or parents. In addition, a tutoring consultation provides an opportunity to collect data that will aid in determining your client's needs. On the other hand, a tutoring interview requires tutors to be well versed in learning theories and tutoring philosophies and to have great interviewing skills. As a result, I have learned how to be prepared for the inevitable in tutoring.

With tutoring interviews, it is not a guarantee that you will be chosen for the job. On the other hand, if you decide to have an in-depth tutoring consultation about how you can help the client, you may charge for this visit. If the client does not want to hire you for their tutoring needs, then you have at least been compensated for your time.

In this chapter, you gained insight into how prospective clients think about tutors and the qualities in which they desire in tutors. In addition, you learned how to master tutoring interviews and tutoring consultations.

CHAPTER 8:
Conducting the Needs Assessment and Developing Instructional Plans

Have you ever been to the doctor when no examinations were done to diagnose your condition? Instead, the doctor simply gave you a diagnosis and sent you on your way. How did you feel? Did you know what was wrong with you? These questions should help you understand how clients feel about their learning progress. Clients want to know what is going on with their learning and what can be done at home to help them improve their skills. Let's look at some data-driven strategies that will help identify your client's needs and tutoring business needs.

How to Conduct a Needs Assessment for Your Tutoring Business

Morrison, Ross, and Kemp (2007) claim, "People are often willing to pay to satisfy expressed needs" (p. 35). Since people are willing to pay for your tutoring services, it is extremely important to use the needs assessment to determine whether the client's expressed needs were valid and could help in formulating goals for his or her individualized tutoring program. In my experience as a tutor, students perform better one-on-one or with small-group instruction that is tailored to their individual needs. Instructional plans are made based upon feedback from parents, clients (adults or students), questionnaires, baseline assessments, and any additional information pertaining to the client.

The purpose of a needs assessment in tutoring is to determine how the tutor can provide individualized instruction to meet the client's needs. After the needs assessment has been completed, the tutor will compile the raw data and communicate the results to the parents (and students, if parents opt to). A targeted needs assessment will be conducted at each consultation. Parents will be asked a series of questions while students are taking their baseline assessment.

The baseline assessment should be no more than twenty-five questions, as clients will tend to lose focus and results may not be reliable. The baseline assessment obviously only reflects the client's current strengths and weaknesses. Once students have received instruction, it would be wise to give another assessment—a progress-monitoring assessment. This type of assessment will be discussed later in this chapter.

SCENARIO: "Let's See What You Need"

India Nicole, an experienced tutor, decided to complete a needs assessment for the eight clients that she had tutored within the first eight months of opening her tutoring business. She noticed that clients came to her needing the same assistance on certain topics. Therefore, she decided that it would be in her best interest to analyze why most clients were coming to her for help with certain topics. India Nicole acknowledged that her targeted population for this needs assessment was clients who ranged from eight to fourteen years old, grades three through eight. Next, she examined each client's baseline assessment, which contained twenty-five questions targeted to his or her grade level. India Nicole understood the importance of reliability and validity, so she had used a variety of strategies to collect data on each client at the tutoring consultation.

Results from the baseline assessment indicated that on objective one (number operations, such as fractions, decimals, prime numbers), seven out of eight clients (88 percent) performed poorly, while four out of eight clients (50 percent) performed poorly on objective two (algebra concepts and patterns). On objective three (geometry concepts), six out of seven (86 percent) performed poorly, while four out of eight clients (50 percent) demonstrated a need to focus on objective four (measurement concepts). Four out of eight clients (50 percent) performed poorly on objective five (probability and statistics), while seven out of eight clients (88 percent) demonstrated a need to focus on objective six (problem solving).

• •

At that point, India Nicole realized that she needed to create or find hands-on lessons to help with the concepts that had challenged a high percentage of clients. She was glad to know where she should spend her time and money when looking to purchase additional resources to help clients.

EXPERT'S ADVICE: The data collection for each client was rather simple, as the tutor triangulated the information so that results were valid and reliable. According to Gay and Airasian (2003), "Researchers triangulate by using different data sources to confirm one another, as when an interview, related documents, and recollections of other participants produce the

> **Expert's Advice** *(continued)*
>
> same descriptions of an event, or when a participant responds similarly to a personal question asked on three different occasions," (p. 215). In the writer's case, triangulation is extremely important to ensure that client's needs are fully detected given that the organization has a track record of being results-oriented. Data revealed the client's strengths and weaknesses so that the tutor could develop an instructional plan to meet the client's needs. Once the instructional plan had been developed, then the results were expressed to parents as soon as possible.

How to Identify Your Clients' Needs

You should make sure that the parent has provided for you the student's name, address, grade level, and previous educational history (e.g., standardized test scores, grade reports, etc.). This information serves as a baseline for developing instructional plans tailored to the client's academic needs. Next, you should construct or buy licensed pre-assessments for the grade level or subject area. It is important to make sure that the state's standards are covered in the pre-assessments. After all, you are trying to increase skills at that specific grade level, as well as increase student achievement on the state assessment. A good place to start is at your state's Department of Education website. For example, in the state of Texas, the Texas Education Agency (TEA) has a website, www.tea.state.tx.us.

A quality pre-assessment will have no more than twenty questions (two or three for each concept or skill). This will allow you to gather rich data about your potential client. Plus, it can help your clients understand why their child may need your tutoring services. Once the client has taken the pre-assessment, it may be a good idea to interview the child to see where he or she may need assistance. Kids are genuine and self-aware of both their proficiencies and deficiencies. Therefore, the information that they provide you is invaluable. Although you may want an adult at each tutoring session, it is important to interview the child alone so that you can get honest and insightful answers. Otherwise, if the child knows that his or her parents are listening to the conversation with you, he or she will not be as open. Prior to the consultation, it may be a good idea to interview the parents with five to ten questions about their child's educational history.

Below are some interview questions for parents to help you get started.

Interview Questions for Parents

1. How is your child's current academic experience?
2. How does your child like to learn?
3. Does your child have a learning disability? If so, what is your child's learning disability?
4. If you answered "YES" that your child has a learning disability, what are the Individualized Education Program(IEP) accommodations?
5. Has your child been retained in school? If so, which grade level(s)?
6. How can I assist your child? What do you expect of an effective tutor?

Please be sure to ask questions about any medications or special accommodations, as you will be responsible for them during your tutoring sessions. Now that you have your information about your client, it's time to develop the instructional plan!

EXPERT'S ADVICE: When I first started tutoring, I realized quickly that it would cost a great deal of money to purchase software that could build pre-assessments for grades K-8. After my second client, I also realized that it would be beneficial to develop my own pre-assessment, as it would save both time and money. That same summer, I decided to develop all math pre-assessments for grades three through eight, since my needs assessments indicated that most of my clients needed assistance at this level.

In addition, I began to develop both progress assessments and skill assessments. For instance, one client may need help determining the coin value of money. For this particular skill, I developed a skills assessment to help ensure that the client mastered the content after instruction. A few weeks later, this skill would be included in the progress-monitoring assessment.

I must forewarn you that creating your own assessments requires a great deal of your time researching, analyzing, and being creative with each test item. It's extremely rewarding, however. Luckily, I enjoy this type of work. If you are working with clients one-on-one, it's a necessity that you create your own assessments or find someone who can create them for you.

Another piece of advice is to save all pre-assessments. The more your business grows, the more clients you will have for whom you will need to create assessments.

> **EXPERT'S ADVICE** *(continued)*
> It would be wise to start looking at each client's situation as a scenario so that you can have rich data to analyze and that you can use to fine-tune your instruction. The bottom line is that you should save all assessments so you can build your own database of quality yet affordable assessments that are tailor made to your clients' needs.

Using Pre- and Post-Assessments with Your Clients

When you receive a new client, you should always start out with a pre-assessment. This is to assess your client's knowledge and skills before treatment. In other words, you want to see where they are before starting your online tutoring program. Once the tutoring program has been completed, then it is deemed appropriate to administer students their post-assessment. At that time, you should be able to compare results to see if your tutoring program was effective for your clients.

Using Licensed Pre- and Post-Assessments to Measure Student Progress

When it comes to ensuring that your assessments are deemed both valid and reliable, it is important to try to use licensed assessments. Another advantage of using licensed assessments is that an answer key typically accompanies these assessments to help with grading them. The disadvantage is that a license product key must be purchased for each assessment or you can purchase the assessment in bulk such as two, five, then, or more assessments.

There are some guidelines that you should consider before purchasing a pre- or post-assessment. These guidelines are as follows:

| **Detailed Feedback** | **Cost-Effective** |

| **Electronic Version Available** |

1. *Detailed Feedback:* When you are providing information to your clients, you want to make sure that it shows how they performed on the assessment. Specifically, you want them to see the areas in which they have mastered and have not mastered. This information benefits both you and the client.
2. *Cost-Effective:* You can pretty much detect a rip-off when you see one. After looking for the benefits of how the product can help you, it should really help you see how it measures up to your budget.
3. *Elective Version Available:* Whether you work with clients face-to-face or online, your tutoring practice will benefit from online assessments. It will save you both time and energy trying to analyze assessments.

These are three guidelines that you should consider when you are in the market for licensed assessments.

> EXPERT'S ADVICE: When using pre- and post-assessments, you should make sure that each client is taking his or her assessment on their own. I highly

> **Expert's Advice** *(continued)*
>
> encourage you to review your client's data to get an idea of what your clients are mastering and not mastering throughout their academic journey.
>
> Last but not least, most clients will ask for this information and as a data-driven tutor, you should be able to provide it to them. Just a heads up, if you plan to expand your tutoring business, then you definitely want to ensure that your clients are being informed and that your tutoring program can be measured. The goal is to stay data driven!

Developing the Instructional Plan

Using the information from the pre-assessment, you should develop an instructional plan that covers math topics for four to five weeks. I have noticed that clients benefit from tutoring when they are able to attend at least two sessions per week. It is key to have lesson plans that can accommodate all learning styles. Whether your client needs help with homework or needs an instructional plan, you should be cognizant of the state-assessment blueprint that covers all student-learning objectives.

This particular client will start off working with prime numbers and progressing to factors, common factors, and greatest common factors in numbers. After the first session, the tutor will place comments in either the "not mastered" or "mastered" column so that parents will be able to see the student's progress with the state standard. This same procedure should be followed with the rest of the sessions outlined in this instructional plan. Please note that monitoring notes should also be taken during the session so that you have more detail about the client's progress. The instructional plan only serves as a roadmap and tool to use for planning instruction.

> **EXPERT'S ADVICE:** Providing clients with an instructional plan is considered a best-tutoring practice. When you are ready to expand your tutoring business, this tutoring practice will come in handy so that you will have written documentation that both you and your client signs prior to beginning the tutoring program. That way, you are not conducting random tutoring sessions. Instead, you will be conducting data-driven tutoring sessions.

Progress-Monitoring Assessments in Tutoring

Progress-monitoring assessments should be given every four to six weeks and should only consist of ten to fifteen questions that cover five to seven concepts. It's important that these assessments are not given too early or too late so that instruction can continue to flow.

There are three benefits of administering progress-monitoring assessments. They are the following:

- **Measure Client's Progress**
- **Complement the Instructional Plan**
- **Assist in Documenting Client's Growth**

The first is that the tutor can ascertain the client's progress. Oftentimes clients will master a skill but later forget it. In the event that this happens, the progress-monitoring assessment will reveal the gap.

The second benefit is that the progress-monitoring assessment can complement the instructional plan. This means that some clients will master all skills on the assessment, but a new area of concern arises from the assessment. For example, a client has problems working with adding and subtracting fractions with unlike denominators. When the tutor looks at the client's thinking (shown work) on the progress-monitoring assessment, the data reveal that this client needs a mini-lesson on finding the least common denominator (LCD) and a review of multiplication and division (facts).

The last benefit of progress-monitoring assessments is that they assist in documenting the student's growth or areas of need. Parents want to see progress over time to ensure that they made the right investment for their child.

> **EXPERT'S ADVICE:** Progress-monitoring assessments are very important to your client's growth. This is the type of assessment that tells how well students are receiving instruction and whether students are able to transfer the knowledge to new situations. If you can, it is important to use electronic assessments for these frequent assessments for your clients.

Setting Goals in Tutoring

Once you have established an area for tutoring, it's important to help clients understand why tutoring is being offered to them and what they can expect to accomplish at each tutoring session.

Many individuals may not view tutoring as a service that should afford students or clients an opportunity to set goals. In fact, tutoring is the best place to set goals, because students are comfortable and can genuinely focus on both personal and learning goals. While the tutor has data that allows him or her to develop an instructional plan, it is equally important for the student to set goals and have concrete evidence that reflects their achievements.

One strategy that tutors can use is reviewing the client's interview questions. Oftentimes students are honest about their goals and will provide insight into their dreams. It may be a good idea to incorporate a few goals into the interview. In other words, interview questions could be designed to capture clients' goals at an early stage in the tutoring relationship. This information can help you plan more effectively to assist students in reaching their goals. I developed five questions that have aided in goal setting for my clients:

Goal-Setting Questions in Tutoring

1. What are your goals for this school year?
2. Where do you see yourself after high school?
3. What can I do to assist you with your goals?
4. What is your class schedule?
5. What do you want to learn? Name something you want to learn in your tutoring sessions.

Question one—*What are your goals for this school year?*—allows clients to share their wishes and future goals, which allows tutors to contribute and/or help them achieve their goals for the school year. For example, I have had several clients who have set goals for the following purposes:

1. Organization
2. Pass state assessment
3. Improve grades in all subjects, especially in math and science

McKeachie and Svinicki (2006) point out, "It is important to remember that we cannot give students goals—they must own their goals" (p. 303). Depending on your role as a tutor, it may be important to set short-term goals for a six-week period, for example. A client might have an issue turning in assignments, for instance, resulting in lower grades. It would therefore benefit the client to set small, attainable goals to increase his or her grade for the next six weeks.

Question two—*Where do you see yourself after high school?*—can help clients understand the purpose of their being in school (and of being tutored). Most importantly, students will be able to see the benefits of education, resulting in more focused tutoring sessions. I believe that everyone is born with a talent, and students tend to search for their talents at a very young age. Thus, tutors can capitalize on students' desires and help them believe in themselves. Imagine working with a client for more than a year and watching him or her transform into that courageous person who can conquer any task. In my ten years of experience, I have been blessed to witness most clients find the strength to conquer. Imagine that! The bottom line is that it is possible, and tutors should capitalize on their clients' long-term goals.

SCENARIO: "I Just Want to Pass Math"

Josephine, a language arts and math tutor, accepted a tutoring job with Jermani, a ten-year-old girl who needed help in mathematics. Jermani had never had As or Bs in math, but always had good grades in reading. Initially, Josephine was having a hard time understanding why this little girl did not comprehend math, when she was an avid reader. Later, Josephine found out that Jermani had a learning disability in math; this had been discovered in third grade, according to her parents' questionnaire. Josephine and Jermani discussed how her tutoring services could help Jermani. During the first tutoring session, the conversation went like this:

Josephine: What are your goals for the remainder of the school year?

Jermani: I want to make at least a B in math the next six weeks and pass my fourth-grade math state assessment for the first time.

Josephine: Okay. What is something you want to learn in your tutoring sessions?

Jermani: I want to learn how to do math. My teachers never showed me how, because I was the last one always finishing my work, and I could not stay after school for help at the time.

Josephine: These goals are achievable, but it will require you to focus a little more in class and ask questions when you are confused. Then, at your tutoring sessions, we can dedicate some time to learning the concepts that you need assistance with in class. Also, we will be working from your instructional plan to help address some of your learning gaps. I expect you to be open and honest with me about your learning. Are you up to the challenge?

Jermani: Yes, I just want to pass math with a good grade and my state assessment so that I can go on to fifth grade next school year.

Tutoring commenced the following day. Jermani's instructional plan required her to come twice a week for the next two months before her state assessment. The day that she took her test, she reported that she was nervous. Her next report card was due to be sent home the following week. At her next session, she showed up with a huge smile on her face and broke the news to Josephine—she had gotten a B in math. This was huge, because she had never had a B before in math. Two weeks later, she had more news to share: she had passed her math state assessment.

At that point, Jermani's parents said that she would be returning for tutoring the following school year. Josephine was happy to learn that Jermani had met her learning goals, but more importantly, Jermani realized that she was capable of doing well in math.

•••

Question three—*What can I do to assist you with your goals?*—allows tutors to meet the expectations of clients. When parents have hired you to work with their child or adult clients have hired you, your main goal as a tutor is to make sure that the client is satisfied with your services and gain insight on how you can assist them. If you are working as an instructional or a strategic tutor, then the instructional plans and monitoring notes should provide you with the necessary information about the client's progress.

Question four—*What is your class schedule?*—pertains to the class schedule of the client. If you are working as a homework tutor, it is crucial for you to have this information so that all assignments can be turned in on time. Also, clients may have a missing assignment or several missing assignments because of an absence, or another legitimate reason. It is therefore the sole responsibility of the tutor to be knowledgeable about missing assignments or deadlines, assuming access has been granted. You are trying to avoid parents from misrepresenting your services. Let's face it: who wants to hire a tutor who is not effective? That's right—no one! Therefore, you should take the initiative to know the client's schedule and other key information for each session.

Question five—*What do you want to learn?*—allows clients to express any concept that they would like to work on so that they can become better at understanding it. While this should be done at the beginning of the first session, this question lends itself to being updated as needed.

In this chapter, you learned how to conduct a needs assessment and develop an instructional plan. You also learned the importance of helping clients set goals in their tutoring sessions and conducting progress-monitoring assessments after several sessions. Now it's time for you to figure out what type of tutor you will need to be for your clients.

CHAPTER 9:
Determining the Type of Tutor You Will Need to Be for Each Tutoring Session

What type of tutor are you? Before you can develop an instructional plan for your client, it is important to identify the type of tutor you will need to be to meet your clients' needs. Let me share with you the three types of tutors: (1) homework tutor, (2) instructional tutor, and (3) strategic tutor.

Three Types of Tutors

Homework Tutor	Instructional Tutor	Strategic Tutor

The Homework Tutor

This type of tutoring requires the tutor to research all the client's school information to help him or her successfully. This information includes teacher information, current grades, and assignment calendars depending on the grade level. Parents sign a release form allowing you, the tutor, to gain access to grades and contact teachers. Please keep in mind that some school districts require that the parents submit a written request to allow a tutor to communicate with teachers about academic matters, such as homework, tests, and projects. To protect yourself and your business, please make sure that you have written consent, as well as your own consent form for clients to sign, especially if you are dealing with children under eighteen or with special needs.

If you are lucky enough to start working with clients at the beginning of the school year or semester, this type of tutoring will seem easy to you. In this case, it is important for you to help the student organize his or her binders or course material for easy navigation.

For example, a client may have a math class binder that needs sections labeled:

TAB 1

TAB 2

TAB 3

TAB 4

TAB 5

Second, the tutor should set personal-learning goals for each tutoring session. I have noticed that clients tend to do a better job when they have a written agreement that can be referred to from time to time. Ultimately, the goal for each client should be to improve his or her skills.

Third, the tutor should set mini-goals to be achieved for each session. For example, if you are working with a client for at least three days, it will be a good idea to have a weekly schedule so that you and the client (and the parents) are fully aware of these sessions.

SCENARIO:
"Not Another Missing Assignment!"

Isabella, a seventh-grade student who is gifted in mathematics, has ADHD and an information-processing disorder. Her parents notice that she has low grades in all her subjects and cannot turn her assignments in on time because her homework is either incomplete or lost. Isabella's parents become frustrated and hire a tutor who can help Isabella with her homework. The tutor's name is Renee.

Renee takes the position (a new way of tutoring for her) and immediately starts working with Isabella. She and Isabella meet three times a week on Tuesdays, Thursdays, and Saturdays. During the first session, Renee realizes that she does not have a clue about Isabella's class assignments and when assignments are due. The only information that is available to her is the assignments that Isabella brought to the session, which is frustrating. This is Renee's first experience being a homework tutor, so she is a little hesitant to ask the parents for more information.

After two weeks, Isabella's situation still does not change—there are still several missing assignments and her grades only improve a little. At that time, Renee has a conference with the parents and asks if she may have permission to contact teachers and/or have access to Isabella's grades. The parents agree to give Renee full access to Isabella's grades, which can be accessed online, since the school district had implemented an online grade book system so that parents are informed about their child's grades in school.

At the end of the grading period, Isabella's grades have improved in all her classes, and she has been missing fewer assignments, thanks to Renee's ability to access her grades in a timely fashion. Also, Renee recommends that she visit with Isabella three times a week, preferably on Tuesdays, Thursdays, and Sundays or Mondays, Tuesdays, and Thursdays. Renee knows that she can better assist Isabella if they meet on those days and have 90-minute or 120-minute sessions.

• •

1. How do you deal with clients who need help with homework and organizational skills?

_____

_____

_____

_____

2. How would you have explained to Isabella's parents the importance of keeping Renee up-to-date with her studies?

_____

_____

_____

_____

> **EXPERT'S ADVICE:** As a homework tutor, you will need to have full access to your client's grades. It would help if parents give you written permission to communicate with the student's teachers. I must forewarn you that most parents will only give you access to grades, and that is fine. Your main focus should be to help the student set weekly and six-week goals to get his or her homework turned in on time and improve his or her grades.
>
> If parents will not give you access to their child's grades or provide a copy of the current grades prior to the tutoring sessions, I strongly encourage you to think twice about accepting the tutoring position. This type of uncooperation will do a disservice to the client and can tarnish your business image or reputation. I have had two clients for whom I was a homework tutor. One client's parents gave me full access, while the other client's parent did not. Therefore, I have learned to implement guidelines for clients when they come to me for homework or study skills assistance.

The Instructional Tutor

The instructional tutor is a tutor who plans instruction according to the client's needs; tutoring lasts anywhere from six weeks to eight months. This type of tutor works with clients who need a minimal amount of assistance on homework. Oftentimes this type of tutor develops an instructional plan to work on skills that need further attention and supplement a student's classroom experience. Most tutors will be this type of tutor. They will learn a lot about their clients because they will be working with the client for at least six weeks at a time. Again, this depends on the client's needs and the instructional plan.

A typical session with an instructional tutor will last thirty minutes to two hours and will follow the same structure as all sessions. You may, however, want to differentiate how the session time is used. For example, for math and science sessions, you may want to schedule at least forty-five minutes to sixty minutes, while an English Language Arts (ELA) session will be ninety minutes to allow for both a reading and writing session. In any event, this type of tutoring will resemble classroom instruction and will hone your teaching/tutoring skills. If you are deciding to enter the classroom or refine your tutoring skills, then this type of tutoring will help you achieve your desires.

SCENARIO: "I'm So Glad We Found You!"

Mahogany Nicole, a physically disabled and hearing-impaired fourth grader, needs help in math has been in and out of school due to her medical conditions since first grade. Her parents have tried helping her and now that she has been promoted to fifth grade, they are looking for a qualified tutor who can help her. Mahogany's dad saw an ad on the bulletin board at a local grocery store and decided to call Kendall, the math tutor who had posted the listing. Kendall asked the parents a series of questions and informed them that she would have to administer a diagnostic assessment prior to working with Mahogany. She also asked them whether they could bring a copy of her Individual Education Plan (IEP) and other academic records.

At the tutoring consultation, Mahogany took the diagnostic assessments, and Kendall told the parents that the next step would be to create an instructional plan for Mahogany. Based upon the diagnostic assessments, it was clear that Mahogany would need at least six weeks of tutoring (twice a week) to cover the gaps from second to fourth grade and work on the fifth- grade concepts. The parents agreed to the instructional plan and pre-paid for both the tutoring consultation and the first six sessions. Mahogany's parents signed a payment agreement stating that the remaining amount would be paid before the seventh tutoring session. The following Monday, Mahogany and Kendall began their first session.

●●●

1. Do you think that this is the ideal client for whom Kendall should work? Why or why not?

_____
_____
_____
_____

2. What additional marketing strategies would you employ to strengthen Kendall's marketing plan? If you would not change anything, why is that so?

_____
_____
_____
_____

The Strategic Tutor

A strategic tutor works with clients who need academic assistance for less than six weeks. In order to serve as a strategic tutor, you must be extremely organized and know which approach to take with each client. As a strategic tutor, it's imperative to have the client complete a pre-assessment. This pre-assessment will give you a better picture of how the client is currently performing in that specific area. In addition to the pre-assessment, it's important to have any school-related data that will provide a history of the client's educational background. Later in this book, you will learn exactly how to develop a pre-assessment or locate one using the Internet.

SCENARIO: "Last-Minute Help"

Sebastian, an undergraduate college student majoring in business, needs to take one course in order to graduate at the end of the semester. He had to take the college entrance exam and failed it by thirty points. Sebastian found out that he needed to improve his college algebra and score a higher grade in order to get into the college algebra course. He started desperately looking online for a tutor because he would take the test again in three days and the class started the following Monday.

He did not have a lot of money, so he was looking for someone who was affordable yet knowledgeable and could help with his immediate math needs. He tried calling several tutors, but only one tutor was available; his name was George. George was booked, but he made time for Sebastian.

Prior to the session, George asked Sebastian to bring his score report and any study material that he had been using. Once he had access to this information, he began to formulate a plan. While the college math course placement exam focused on higher math (calculus, trigonometry, etc.), it was smarter to focus on the basic math and progress to the college algebra. Therefore, George designed mini-lessons that mainly covered college algebra but also had to include the basic math so that the client could understand why the process was needed. In other words, it was equally important to cover the basic math concepts so that the client could understand how some of the mathematical processes at a higher level worked and how they built upon the basic mathematical concepts. After a couple of two-hour sessions, Sebastian had acquired all the skills he needed to be proficient, and time had run out for him—the test was the next day.

George was concerned because he knew that more sessions were needed. The following week, Sebastian called George to tell him that he had scored high enough to be eligible to take his college algebra class and would be graduating soon. Sebastian thanked George for making time for him and said that he would come again or recommend him to others. George was extremely happy and realized that he might be able to do it again with other clients.

1. If you were in this situation, would you have serviced this client? Why or why not?

_____
_____
_____
_____
_____

2. If you could interview George, what type of questions would you ask him? Why?

_____
_____
_____
_____

> **EXPERT'S ADVICE:** I would not recommend that tutors take on a tutoring job like this unless they are sure that they can fulfill the client's needs. If so, these types of jobs will boost your reputation and clientele. Also, you will find that a lot of clients will come to you at the last minute for test prep. If you can successfully help clients at the last minute, you will be accomplished as a tutor—just don't forget to write down your strategies to refine them for the next client who may need assistance with the same test or skill.

Tutoring Archetypes That Work Best with High School and Adult Learners

Harootunian and Quinn (2008) identify and describe three tutor archetypes: (1) the pragmatist, (2) the architect, and (3) the surveyor (p. 15). These tutor archetypes are commonly used with high school and adult learners, but, depending on your teaching style, you may be able to incorporate these archetypes with younger learners.

Tutoring Archetypes for High School and Adult Learners

The Pragmatist Tutor	The Architect Tutor	The Surveyor Tutor

The Pragmatist Tutor

"The pragmatist views tutoring as a series of organized events. These type of tutors ask a variety of 'why' questions designed to help tutees [clients] focus on the steps needed to solve the problems," (Harootunian & Quinn, 2008, p. 15). In other words, pragmatist tutors like to have a structured tutoring session. Pragmatist tutors have an objective for the lesson, just like a teacher.

The tutoring styles of pragmatist tutors include the following:

1. Advocates for strong work ethic
2. Favors worksheets and regular practice
3. Uses a questioning technique that involves direct answers
4. Communicates mostly during dialogues with the tutees (Harootunian & Quinn, 2008, p. 16).

This type of tutoring should be limited when conducting tutoring sessions. It focuses on the tutor rather than the client, whereas clients should experience most of the learning process. Harootunian and Quinn (2008) warn, "[P]roviding everything for tutees [doing all the work for clients] is not effective and should be reconsidered" (p.16). In other words, tutors who choose the pragmatist tutoring approach will be doing a disservice to clients and their tutoring business's reputation may be at stake. So, don't jeopardize everything you have worked hard for by being this type of tutor.

•••

SCENARIO: "I'm Still Confused"

Emily, a bona fide tutor, has been tutoring for over ten years. She has mastered being a tutor but has recently noticed declining passing rates for her clients. She believes that learners should figure stuff out for themselves, just like she had to do. At each session, she gives out worksheets and does all the talking during discussion time.

1. How can Emily improve her tutoring sessions?

_____
_____
_____
_____

2. What are some additional strategies that Emily can employ to help with engaging her learners?

_____
_____
_____
_____

> **EXPERT'S ADVICE:** In Emily's case, she seems to have forgotten what it took to be a well respected tutor. I would recommend that Emily explore or even blend some of the other tutor archetypes to accommodate her clients' needs. By using worksheets and dominating the learning opportunities, Emily is doing an injustice to her clients. While I am not saying those worksheets are "bad," there are so many more strategies that can be used to teach her clients. Emily must not forget that her clients may have a learning style different from her own, and she needs to cater to their needs and not hers.

The Architect Tutor

"The architect views the study of math as finding pieces of information that create the steps necessary to solve a particular problem" (Harootunian and Quinn, 2008, p. 16). In other words, this type of tutor focuses on making sure that the clients understand; then he or she follows up with higher-level questions, such as why, how, and what. The tutoring styles of architect tutors are the following:

1. Scaffolds [guides] students to help them gain a better understanding, which is followed by strategically crafted questions.
2. Uses diagrams (visuals) to help clients make connections between concepts.
3. Uses questioning strategies that are followed by a new level of inquiry when clients respond.
4. Uses a particular problem-solving style to solve problems.
5. Uses the tutees' responses to determine their learning styles and abilities and conducts sessions in a manner that best supports the client (Harootunian & Quinn, 2008, p. 17).

Although the characteristics of the architect tutor emphasize math, this approach can be applied to any subject. The architect approach lends itself to asking highly effective questions and truly helps clients grasp the material.

Harootunian and Quinn (2008) say it best: "The client's goal in classes is not to get good grades or pass tests, but to learn the material. By setting that as a goal, it then helps him or her achieve the grades and test scores that he or she wants," (p. 17). This description from a client's perspective is powerful, and tutors need to revisit why they chose a certain tutoring approach in the first place.

SCENARIO: "I Got It Now!"

Mercedes, a well respected tutor in her community, accepted a client who needed help with geometry. Joe, the client, did not have anything available to the tutor, other than his grade report. Mercedes asked him what he needed assistance with, and he told her working with right triangles in a problem-solving context. Mercedes knew immediately that he meant trigonometry. She then showed Joe a word problem that contained an image of a right triangle where one leg of the triangle was a flagpole. The question required Joe to find the length from the ground to the top of the flagpole. Once Joe acknowledged that this was the type of question with which he needed assistance, she began to ask a series of questions.

By the end of the session, Joe was working problems independently, but he still had questions about some of the problems. Mercedes continued to ask questions that sparked thinking about how and why he chose to solve the problems the way that he did, while also encouraging Joe to use the visuals provided in the problem or to construct his own. Joe made a three out of four on his mini-assessment at the end of the tutoring session. Mercedes told him to keep up the great work and that he would do fine on this material.

1. What strategies did Mercedes employ in her tutoring session with Joe that made it a successful session?

_____
_____
_____
_____

2. How do you find out what your clients need in such a short time, if an assessment is not given?

_____
_____
_____
_____
_____

3. Do you use the same strategy as Mercedes? Why or why not?

_____
_____
_____
_____
_____

> **Expert's Advice:** Mercedes provided a tutoring environment that allowed her client, Joe, to feel comfortable to make mistakes, yet she asked effective questions that guided him in the right direction. Mercedes knew that Joe had background knowledge with right triangles, but she helped him think about everyday objects and how they relate to some aspect of math. Joe had to make a visual image of how a flagpole may look; this visual helped him understand how to solve problems and use common sense to answer the problem. I believe that Mercedes' approach to tutoring helped her client. These strategies were definitely data-driven and catered to the client. Did you notice that Mercedes used a worksheet to

> **Expert's Advice** *(continued)*
>
> assess Joe's needs? In this setting, worksheets are fine because you need to have a quantitative measure to assess your client's needs. Most tutoring sessions will require this archetype, especially if you are an instructional tutor. Again, this solely depends on your client's needs.
>
> The bottom line is you must first determine what your clients' needs are and then choose the best tutoring model to fit them. It may be that you have to blend some of the models to meet your clients' needs, so you need to look at all types of tutors and choose carefully.

The Surveyor Tutor

"The surveyor examines a subject's terrain and creates maps, charts, and diagrams to provide his tutees with visual representations of the landscape" (Harootunian and Quinn, 2008, p. 17). In other words, this type of tutor focuses on looking at the big picture of a concept and then makes both a mental map of approaching the concept and a visual for helping clients make sense of the concepts.

The tutoring styles of surveyor tutors are the following:

1. Prefers unstructured tutoring format and lets the tutees' needs and questions guide the direction of the tutoring session.
2. Places greater emphasis on assisting them to discover the correct aspects of math theory to apply to each problem.

3. Concentrates much of his or her energies and talents on figuring things out.
4. Demonstrates a calm demeanor and a willingness to approach each tutoring session as representing a new set of ideas that need to be understood.
5. Uses questions that are open and spontaneous, created to fit the terrain of each learning situation.
6. Engages the tutees in an articulate manner and strives for balance and conceptual understanding, often taking many steps to solve problems.
7. Prefers the team approach to learning (Harootunian and Quinn, 2008, pp. 17-18).

After looking at each type of tutor and the tutoring archetypes, it is very important for tutors to ask themselves how to determine their tutoring purpose for each client. This can be done by assessing the client's needs at the tutoring consultation. That way, you can quickly identify the type of tutor(s) that you may need to be to ensure that the client meets his learning goal(s) while attending your tutoring practice.

In this chapter, you examined the various types of tutors, along with their tutoring styles. Also, you learned that you would need to choose the tutoring model that best fits your tutoring style yet meets the client's needs. Now it's time to take a look at how to conduct tutoring sessions.

CHAPTER 10:
Conducting Tutoring Sessions and Writing Monitoring Notes for Clients

You have just gotten either your first client or have been in business for a while. At this point, it is time to analyze how to conduct your tutoring sessions. It seems like it should be a piece of cake, but there is a little more to it than you may first believe. In this section, we will be discussing how to develop procedures for opening and closing tutoring sessions. Before we do this, we need to take a look at the Tutoring Framework for Effective Tutoring.

The Tutoring Framework for Effective Tutoring

Before engaging in tutoring sessions, it is very important to understand the framework that makes up an effective tutoring session. Let's take a look at the following model:

Dr. Alicia Holland's Tutoring Framework for Effective Tutoring Model

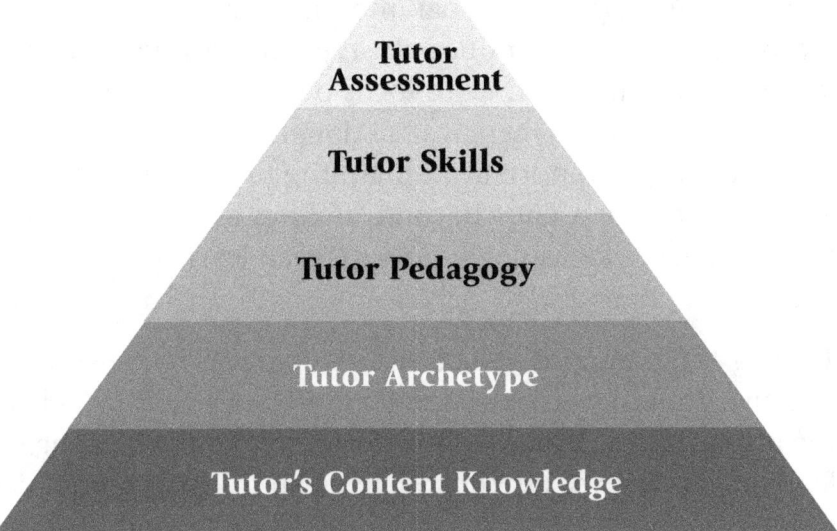

When it comes to the *Tutor's Content Knowledge*, it is very important to understand that a tutor's content knowledge is the foundation of the tutoring session because he or she knows the direction the tutoring session needs to flow. In this figure, it is at the bottom layer because it represents the basis in which the tutoring pyramid needs to be strong. In other words, tutors need to have strong content knowledge to be able to help others learn and grow.

In terms of the *Tutor Archetype*, they are the various types of tutor styles a tutor can utilize to help their learners. Dr. Alicia Holland (2010) identifies and describes three types of tutors: homework tutors, instructional tutors, and strategic tutors (p. 74). These tutor types are associated with working with K-12 learners (Holland-Johnson, A., 2010).

As mentioned in the previous chapter, Harootunian and Quinn (2008) identify and describe three tutor archetypes that work best with high school and adult learners. These three tutor archetypes are the following: (a) the pragmatist; (b) the architect; and (c) the surveyor (p. 15).

The *Tutor Pedagogy* is also paramount for effective tutoring. Once tutors have determined the type of tutoring they need for their learners, it is time to focus on "how" they will tutor the learners. This is where instructional strategies and learning theories are important in planning tutoring sessions for learners. This step goes beyond looking at learning objectives, but really focusing on how to reach learners using best practices.

Tutoring Skills are also valued in this tutoring framework for effective tutoring. At this point, tutors are ready to deliver the instruction to learners. It is the job of the tutor to engage learners and deliver instruction using all learning modalities to increase the chances of learners retaining the information. When learners retain the information, they are able to apply it to a new situation or current learning situation.

Last but not least, the *Tutor Assessment* is there to determine if the learner has benefitted from effective tutoring. In other words, once the tutor and learner have worked together on concepts, the tutor should provide assessments to measure the learner's mastery of skills. These assessments should not be comprehension questions only, but a variety of questions that will enable the learner to truly reflect their knowledge. Tutors must implement an assessment plan that will capture immediate and future retention of the learners' knowledge. Tutors who have a strong content knowledge will be able to create or provide various types of assessments to meet the learners' needs and depict a true assessment of the learners' knowledge and skills.

> **EXPERT'S ADVICE:** When you study this framework for effective tutoring, please take the time to reflect on why I focused on the improvement of tutoring your skills at the beginning of the book. Since you see that the tutor's knowledge is crucial, it is very important to be a life-long learner so that your clients can reap the benefits.
>
> When you take some time out to study your competition, what do you notice? Are they steadily getting clients because of low prices or is it because the tutor delivers results for his or her clients? I will let you be the judge. My challenge to you is to always consider your approach to learning as a life-long journey. The truth is that we all learn something new each day and the same occurs in the tutoring industry.

How to Open Tutoring Sessions

Each tutoring session should open with a greeting to make a connection with the client. After a connection has been made, you should communicate with the client what he or she will be learning and address any goals that have been set, whether the goals are for this session or another session. By communicating the session's objective(s), the tutor allows the client to be prepared for what the session will cover. Imagine going to the dentist's office if the dentist never told you what was going to go on in that visit. The most you may know about the visit is that your teeth will be cleaned. If any other procedures were performed, wouldn't you be upset? The same is true for your clients; they want to be in the know about their learning.

> ### Sample Opening of a Tutoring Session
>
> *Tutor:* Hi, my name is Zoey, and I will be your tutor today. How was your day?
>
> *Student:* My day was okay. I lost my favorite pendant in gym. Other than that, I am good. Here's my report card.
>
> *Tutor:* In today's session, we are going to look at describing quadrilaterals according to their characteristics. Have you worked with quadrilaterals before?
>
> *Student:* Yes, I remember working with squares and rectangles a lot in fourth and fifth grade. Isn't that what quadrilaterals are?
>
> *Tutor:* Well, you have identified two quadrilaterals. The mathematical definition is: Quadrilaterals are polygons that have four sides. It's great to know that you already know about squares and rectangles, because you will find yourself having fun learning the rest of the quadrilaterals. I noticed that you met your goal of receiving at least a B in your math class. Based upon your report card grades, you are doing well in all your classes. You got an A in your math class. Great job; keep up the good work.

Once you have opened the session, it is time to personalize the session and begin working on your client's specific needs. We will talk about ways to praise clients during the tutoring sessions later in this chapter.

How to Close Tutoring Sessions

As with any presentation, you want to end it with a sense that your audience has gotten the importance of the message. The same is true for a tutoring session; a tutoring session should be brought to an educationally sound close. What does "educationally sound" mean? This means that you should not be in the middle of a question and abruptly stop the session because of time constraints. This leaves the session open, and neither you nor the client can determine what the next steps may be for the next session. On the other hand, if there was a written assessment or monitoring notes, then the tutor should be able to pick up where he or she and the client left of, and the client has an idea of the topics that will be covered in the next tutoring session. Please keep in mind that all sessions are not going to be the same and will eventually need to come to an end.

Sample Closing of a Tutoring Session

Tutor: You did a great job on your homework. Now, let me grade your mini-assessment on comparing fractions. While I look at these five questions, take a moment to stretch, or you may play Math Man [an online educational game that allows individuals to practice their multiplication skills] on the computer.

Student: Okay, I think I will stretch as I am standing up to go play Math Man.

Tutor: Okay, Mike. You have five minutes, and then I need you to come back to the table so we can discuss your results and end the session. (Five minutes have passed.)

Student: I'm back. What did I make on my assessment?

Tutor: You scored a six out of eight, which is 75 percent. This score lets me know that we can move on to the next topic. You did a great job today. Do you have any questions? What did you learn in today's session?

Student: No, I do not have any questions. I learned that I can cross- multiply or find a common denominator to compare fractions.

> *Tutor:* If you do not have any further questions, then this session has ended, and if there's still time, you can continue working on your multiplication skills until your ride comes. See you next week.
>
> *Student:* Okay. Bye and thank you.

> **EXPERT'S ADVICE:** As you may already know, the beginning and ending of a tutoring session are important. I must admit that when I first started my tutoring business I had to learn how to start a tutoring session, even though I had teaching experience. Tutoring sessions open differently from a lesson that would be taught in class. Please understand that clients feed off your energy. After all, you are running a business (one that you love), and clients want to learn from an energetic and positive person. The main concept about opening and closing tutoring sessions is that the feelings experienced during this time will affect: (1) the climate during the tutoring session, and (2) whether or not the client will be motivated to come again. Think about it—would you want to return to a business where no one greets you or appears jovial? Would you want to return to a business that didn't thank you or show you that you are important? Well, your clients don't either... that's why it is important to devise a strategy for opening and closing your tutoring sessions.

Structure of Tutoring Sessions

A typical tutoring session, whether you are a homework, instructional, or strategic tutor, would last forty-five minutes to two hours. Some clients prefer to work in two-hour increments to complete homework and other assignments. Oftentimes this works for motivated and older clients. This allows them to devote focused time to homework. Here are suggested pacing schedules for a typical tutoring session lasting one hour or two hours.

- 5-10 minutes   Open session
- 25 minutes   Subject 1
- 25 minutes   Subject 2
- 25 minutes   Subject 3
- 25 minutes   Subject 4
- 5-10 minutes   Close session

Please keep in mind that tutoring sessions should be tailored to your client's needs. For instance, if you have a client with special needs, more time may be spent on one or two subjects, depending on his or her comfort level. In any event, these pacing schedules only serve as a starting point for structuring tutoring sessions.

Praising Student Motivation and Performance in Tutoring Sessions

How many people do you know who would turn down praise? Have you ever been praised for a job well done? What does praise mean to you?

According to the online Merriam-Webster dictionary (2012), to praise is "To express a favorable judgment of" (para. 1).

Here are a few questions to consider when praising clients:

1. How do your clients respond to praise?

2. Do you use verbal or nonverbal praises? How do you use them?

3. Have you thought about a reward system? Why or why not?

4. How does praise look in tutoring?

Tutors may choose to praise students either verbally or non-verbally. Verbal praises are thoughts spoken in real time. For example, "Nice job" or "You are doing great" are verbal praises. In tutoring, these types of praises are warranted, but praises should be more specific for individual clients' achievements. Imagine that you have received praise from your boss, but he only said to you, "Nice job!" How would that feel? Initially, you would be feeling good inside to the point that you were glowing. Once your brain had processed the information, however, you would be asking yourself, "What did I do a nice job on?" The point is that you are spending time and energy on trying to figure out what your boss is praising you for when you should be putting the energy toward your job responsibilities. Do you want your clients to have the same experience? Praise does not mean anything if it is given either in isolation or too often. Praise works best when it is linked to a specific task or behavior. Gonzalez- Mena (2009) says it best:

They [Adults] replace honest feedback with constant overblown praise. Praise is no cure for low self-esteem. All it does is create a need for the child to look to the adult for a judgment of everything he does—if you overdo praise, your words become meaningless (p. 211).

SCENARIO: "Yes, You Can"

Daisy, a tenth-grade student who has dyslexia and dysgraphia, has been working with a private reading tutor named Josh. Daisy has difficulty comprehending complex information, especially if the information pertains to specific subject areas. After Josh worked with Daisy for five months, she finally passed the tenth-grade reading test. When he heard the news, Josh called Daisy's parents and congratulated them. He also talked with Daisy, telling her, "Daisy, you have been working so hard on your reading skills and all your hard work paid off. Congratulations, and I am so proud of you. Keep up the great work."

From that point on, Daisy continued to work with Josh once a week and continued to improve her reading skills and confidence in learning.

1. Is there anything that you would have done differently? Why or why not?

_____
_____
_____
_____
_____

2. How do you praise your clients in your tutoring services?

_____
_____
_____
_____
_____

> **EXPERT'S ADVICE:** Josh did a great job with being specific in his praise of Daisy. The praise actually worked in this situation. Specific praise can go a long way with people if it is genuine and consistent.

Reward Systems in Tutoring

Clients need to be rewarded for engagement and performance so that they are able to feel confident about their learning.

There are several strategies that can be used to reward clients. One strategy that can be used as a reward system is the ticket system, while other strategies that can enhance a reward system include both gift cards and small gifts.

Using the Tickets to Enhance Your Reward System in Your Tutoring Practice

The ticket system should be designed to reward desired performance and effort. Tickets should be given each session, but no more than five tickets should be handed out in a single one-hour session. This is because you do not want clients to expect to receive rewards for every little task. Think about your own reward credit cards, customer reward cards (e.g., store reward cards), or merit raises. Do you constantly receive rewards without working hard for them? If you do, please let me know so that I can sign up to receive these rewards as well!

Here's a sample ticket system and the way it works.

Students can earn up to five tickets in a session and can cash their tickets in at any time.

Students can earn tickets the following ways:

- 100 percent on a mini-assessment = three tickets
- 90 percent to 99 percent on a mini-assessment = two tickets
- 80 percent to 89 percent on a mini-assessment = one ticket
- Motivation = discretion of tutor
- Participation = discretion of tutor
- Good grades in school (per six or nine weeks) = ten tickets

- Turning in all assignments on time (must have teacher's signatures) = five tickets
- Good test grades = three tickets per test in every subject

What Can You Buy with Your Tickets?

- Five tickets: small items, such as pens, pencils, erasers, stickers.
- Ten tickets: medium items, such as playing cards, extra time on the computer to play game of choice, other items that are donated.
- Fifteen tickets: large items, such as games that are donated.
- Twenty-five tickets: free movie ticket of choice, other items that are donated.
- One hundred tickets: large items that are donated, such as free iTunes card, or $25 gift card.
- Five hundred tickets: iPod, video game of choice, or $50 gift card.
- One thousand tickets: mini-laptop computer, video game system of choice, or $100 gift card.
- Monthly drawing for a prize: at the end of each month (TBD).

> **EXPERT'S ADVICE:** I must admit that at first I was a little hesitant to add such a system to reward desired performance and effort. In fact, for the first three years, I did not have an official reward system. I instituted it because a parent had recommended it and supplied me with costly items that students could purchase with their earned tickets. When I introduced the reward system to both parents and clients, the

> **EXPERT'S ADVICE** *(continued)*
>
> response was overwhelmingly positive. At that moment, I realized that I was moving in the right direction. The hard parts were determining the frequency of when to give out tickets, management of the ticket system, and choosing criteria for the system.
>
> I strongly recommend that you explain to clients (and parents) the rationale of the ticket system and link it to research. That way there will not be any misunderstandings, and the expectations will be clear. This can be done in person, but I strongly suggest that you send it via e-mail or place it in your newsletter to your clients. If you use this system appropriately, you will be content with the results.

Using Small Gifts and Gift Cards to Enhance Your Reward System in Your Tutoring Practice

When it comes to providing gifts to clients, it is very important to make sure that you follow a few guidelines that will keep your tutoring reputation out of trouble.

Below are a few guidelines to ensure that you are making the right decisions in the best interest of your clients.

Inexpensive Gift	Education-Related	Specific Timeframe

When it comes to the first guideline, *Inexpensive Gift,* you really have to be careful. You are in business to help others.

Therefore, you main goal should not be to entice clients to sign up with you for tutoring services because you offer a special gift. As a result, you should make sure that the value does not exceed $50. Instead, you want to make sure that you provide an incentive so that clients will show up to their tutoring sessions. The fact that they will receive a gift valued at $50 is a blessing. Honestly, there are a great deal of gifts that can be purchased and still be meaningful to your clients.

The second guideline, *Education-Related*, is also important for your tutoring business credibility. You do not want to find yourself giving out gifts that you cannot justify on how it will help your client's education. Therefore, you need to research gifts that are beneficial to your clients.

The third guideline, *Providing a Specific Timeframe*, lets the client know how they can be eligible for their free gift and when it will be available to redeem. Typically, once clients are enrolled, then they are notified that they are eligible depending on the completion of their tutoring program.

Once students have completed their program, then they will be notified when gifts have been mailed out or can be picked up at the office.

> **EXPERT'S ADVICE:** I provided you with some good guidelines for keeping within the integrity of your tutoring program. If you plan on expanding your tutoring practice, then you will need to keep prices at or below $50, especially if you plan on working with the government. They frown on tutoring businesses who offer big-ticket gifts such as iPads and computers. Honestly, I do not blame them because our job is to

> **EXPERT'S ADVICE** *(continued)*
>
> educate, not bribe people. However, you can offer to purchase learning tools for your clients, which is a totally different story.
>
> I think that a rewards system should be viewed as an added benefit of why clients choose you, and you should treat it as such.
>
> In terms of gift cards, you need to follow the same guidelines. If you are out of ideas, ask your clients by finding out their interests and favorite books. With this type of information, you cannot go wrong—it does not get any better than that.

Writing Monitoring Notes for Clients during Tutoring Sessions

Let's take a look at a tutoring situation with Amy, a reading tutor.

SCENARIO: "How is My Child Doing?" "He's Doing Fine."

Amy, a reading tutor, has been tutoring for two years now. She only works with three clients per year because she is only supplementing her income. Each of her clients has been with her at least a year. She meets each of them at their home. On one particular Tuesday, one of the clients asked how his son was doing. Rather than give detailed notes, Amy communicated his progress verbally.

Two weeks later, the parent attended a parent/teacher conference and discovered that his son was performing poorly in reading. The parent did not have any documentation from Amy to show the teacher that he was making progress. Immediately, the parent called Amy and informed him of his grades. In addition, the parent fired Amy as his child's tutor because there was not any written evidence that she was an effective tutor.

• •

1. What could Amy have done differently in this situation?

_____
_____
_____
_____
_____

2. How would you have handled the situation with this parent?

_____
_____
_____
_____
_____

3. From the parent's perspective, do you think that he made the right decision? Why or why not?

_____
_____
_____
_____
_____

> **EXPERT'S ADVICE:** This could have been prevented by taking monitoring notes. Typically, students who are having problems in school will perform better in tutoring because of the setting. This was an opportunity for Amy to show her skills as an effective tutor by being proactive. Parents need to know how their child is performing.
>
> You also have to be careful because there are some parents out there that will sue you for professional liability so you it is always in your best interest to have insurance and document like crazy.

Imagine submitting an assignment to your teacher, and she does not provide feedback. How would you feel? Or, imagine that you applied for a loan and did not receive feedback on why you were denied. How would you feel? That is how clients feel when they do not have updates on either their progress or their child's progress. Monitoring notes serve three purposes.

1. They help keep track of the client's progress.
2. They help keep you fully informed about instructional decisions.
3. They keep clients (and parents) informed of their (or their child's) progress.

Monitoring notes allow tutors and parents to have documentation of student learning. There are some components that must be included in order for monitoring notes to be useful to both clients and the tutor. These components are the following: (1) student and session information; (2) effort/attitude; (3) student progress; (4) next instructional step(s); (5) parent resources, if any; and (5) upcoming sessions/request for parent-tutor conference.

Student and Session Information	Effort/Attitude	Student Progress
Next Instructional Step(s)	Parent Resources	Upcoming Sessions/Request for Parent-Tutor Conference

Student and Session Information

Student and session information provide critical information to help identify clients and keep records accurate. The student information should include the client's name and date of birth, though I only use the date of birth when I have more than one client with the same first and last name. The session information should clearly state the subjects tutored and the date/time of the tutoring session. All this information should be written at the beginning of the monitoring notes for easy reference.

Effort/Attitude

This component is extremely important for tutoring sessions. It provides vital information to help you improvise for the tutoring session. In other words, when a client is happy and motivated to learn, then your energy will be high and the tutoring session will go well. On the other hand, if the client is not happy about coming to the session, then you will have to be creative to get the session going. Please understand that clients are paying for your services, and they expect you to provide quality services to them, despite the fact that their child does not want to meet with you.

SCENARIO: "I Don't Wanna Be Here—Take Me Away, Now!"

Ethan, a fifth grader who has attention-deficit hyperactivity disorder (ADHD) and an information-processing disorder, just learned that he had to attend private tutoring in math. Ethan also attended after-school math tutoring at his school twice a week. His mother found a tutor online named Matt.

Upon arriving at the tutoring session, Ethan's mother warned the tutor that Ethan was upset about attending the session. Matt, a novice tutor, was grateful for the alert because he had time to adjust the opening of his session with Ethan. At the beginning of the tutoring session, Ethan told Matt that he was mad because he was not able to play his video game during his free time because he had to come see him for tutoring. The session did continue, but Matt had to link the lesson to Ethan's favorite sport—football. Ethan had joined the community flag football team and would have his first game the following week. To Matt' advantage, he used that information to increase Ethan's motivation for the tutoring session. This strategy worked, resulting in a productive tutoring session.

1. If you were in Matt's situation, how would you have handled the situation?

_____
_____
_____
_____

2. What type of recommendation would you provide to parents regarding scheduling their child during extracurricular activities?

_____

_____

_____

_____

Student Progress

This component will detail how the client performed during the session. It should be in narrative form, but succinct, so that you are able to get an overall picture of the client's strengths and weaknesses during the session. If any mini-assessments are given at the end of the session, you should include the results. For example, a client named Shirley got three out of four test questions correct, which is 75 percent. As a result, Shirley has mastered how to compare fractions using concrete objects.

A short paragraph (three to five sentences) should be included in this section for each subject that you are working on. For instance, if you are working on math and reading skills, there should be a section clearly labeled "Math and Reading," followed by the name of the activity or skill so that clients can understand the information. This is important because parents or guardians or adult clients are responsible for payment. Once this section has been completed, you should list the next instructional step(s).

Next Instructional Step(s)

In this section, you should put the next steps for clients, which will be determined based upon their performance in the session. In other words, if the client has mastered a skill, then he or she should progress to the next skill indicated on the instructional plan. On the other hand, if a client has not mastered a concept, there should be an opportunity to revisit the concept either in the same session, given that time permits, or in the next tutoring session. Once this section has been completed, you should list additional resources for parents or adult clients.

Parent Resources

Parents and adult clients are always looking for additional resources to help their child to practice a skill at home. As their private tutor, you should be committed to providing services beyond tutoring sessions. As Maya Angelou puts it, "I've learned that people will forget what you said, people will forget what you did, but people will never forget how you made them feel." In other words, people will remember your services because of how you made them feel. Therefore, it is crucial to provide quality tutoring sessions, and excellent customer service will keep clients coming or referring others to you. Depending on your relationship with your clients, they will let you know if they need additional assistance at home. Some clients, however, are afraid to ask for additional resources because they may fear that it will cost more money. By providing additional resources, you are empowering clients to further their studies in their targeted areas.

Upcoming Sessions/Request for Parent-Tutor Conference

This section lends itself to reminding clients about their upcoming sessions so that they can make note of them. While this section provides a reminder, it is also a good idea to send an e-mail or text message or make a phone call to help clients remember their sessions. In addition, this section can be used to request parent-tutor conferences. In any event, monitoring notes allow for both clients and tutors to stay "in the know" about their needs and appointments.

> **EXPERT'S ADVICE:** Monitoring notes can be considered part of the lifeblood of your tutoring business because they are so valuable. If you supply your clients with detailed monitoring notes, they will feel (and have proof) that your services are helping them or their child. In addition, if you have the intention of expanding your business or applying to professional tutoring organizations, then it is in your best interest to provide thorough monitoring notes. After all, you are accountable for the client's learning while he or she is receiving your tutoring services.
>
> When it comes to working as a homework tutor, you still need to document progress. This is done by taking monitoring notes, just like you would if you assumed the role of other types of tutors.
>
> The bottom line is that monitoring notes are considered data driven because it helps tell the story of a learner's academic situation. For instance, both tutors and parents are able to review the learner's (and their child's) progress over time. Therefore, it is very important to understand that monitoring notes capture both quantitative and qualitative data. Nevertheless, monitoring notes are considered a great tool to help understand and improve each learner's academic achievement.

Using Tutoring Session Time Cards for Tutoring Sessions

How do you know when a learner is out of tutoring sessions? Each school year, it is very important to keep track of the number of sessions that a client has attended. You may be wondering what type of information should be kept on a session card. Don't worry. I will share that with you.

The items that should be collected on the tutoring session time cards are listed below.

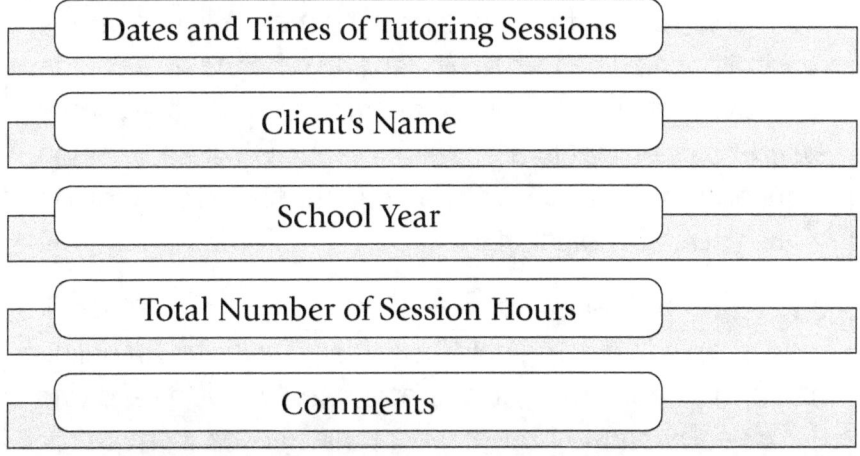

1. <u>Dates and Time of Tutoring Sessions</u>: This can be done in semesters, including the summer semester or in months of the year. Depending on how you want to display this information, you can add both. Whatever you decide, it should also include the specific day and time of the tutoring session.

2. <u>Client's Name</u>: You need to have the client's name or reference code listed to adequately document and file the learner's progress.

3. <u>School Year</u>: This is important if this is a returning client from a previous school year.

4. <u>Total Number of Session Hours</u>: You want to have this information readily available so that you can collect data on when clients are typically enrolled in your tutoring practice.

5. <u>Comments</u>: This section comes in handy if you need to document when payment is due again for services. Any comments listed in this section should pertain to the client and the tutoring sessions.

> **EXPERT'S ADVICE:** Tutoring session cards are great for many reasons. After working with many clients, many parents call the office regarding the next session or payment for tutoring sessions. Also, they may need to reschedule a session or there was a session cancellation. Whatever the reason, tutoring session cards are the solution.
>
> Last but not least, please print them on cardstock and staple them to their file folder. If you run an online tutoring business, you will still need to do the same process because you may not always be in front of your computer when parents call about tutoring session changes.

Providing Student's Additional Practice After Tutoring Sessions

After working with clients, you may discover that they will need additional practice after tutoring sessions. Depending on how frequently the learner attends sessions, it will also depend on how you will assign student's additional practice. No matter the situation, you should follow a few guidelines to ensure that this additional practice benefits the learner.

Below are some guidelines to follow when providing student's additional practice after tutoring sessions:

| Clear Directions | Recommended Schedule | Due Date |

| Signature Box | Tutor Comments |

1. **Provide Clear Directions:** You have to understand that you will not be present when the learner is completing the work.

2. **Include a Recommended Schedule:** You need to let the learner know how to pace himself or herself. For example, if you provide five learning activities, then you should stress the importance of completing one learning activity per day and explain your rationale in a kid-friendly fashion.

3. **Highlight the Due Date:** You want to communicate when the tutoring practice packet is due. That way, there are not any surprises.

4. **Add a Parent/Guardian Signature Box:** When working with K-12 learners, you should always keep the parent both informed and engaged. That way, they also share the responsibility of ensuring that their child is completing the tutoring packet.

5. **Provide Tutor Comments:** You should always leave tutor comments to indicate what is going on with the packet. This type of feedback should be about the tutoring practice packet only, not the actual student work.

Examples of comments can include that the parent did not sign or the packet was turned in late or incomplete.

By following these guidelines, you are able to properly assign additional practice for your clients.

> **Expert's Advice:** Tutoring practice packets are great to supplement tutoring sessions. However, you may not use them a lot during the academic school year. I found a lot of success with them during summer tutoring sessions.
>
> If you are working with home-schooled students, then you will use these packets a lot to ensure that students are getting the appropriate amount of practice to master the skill.
>
> You can find these forms and additional resources at www.becomingabettertutorblog.com to help with your tutoring business needs.

In this chapter, you learned how to open and close tutoring sessions and how to structure your tutoring sessions. Also, you learned the value of praise in tutoring sessions and how to write monitoring notes for clients to document their progress. Last but not least, you had an opportunity to learn about the Tutoring Framework for Effective Tutoring and how to use both session cards and tutoring practice packets with your clients. In the next chapter, you will take what you have learned about tutoring into the classroom.

Part V:
Taking Tutoring to the Classroom: Combining Classroom Teaching and Tutoring

CHAPTER 11:
Tutoring Strategies: A Way to Increase Student Achievement in the Classroom

If you are reading this last chapter, this means that you are thinking about tutoring in the classroom or becoming a teacher, or you are already a teacher looking for strategies to increase student achievement. As you are reading through this chapter, ask yourself the following questions:

1. What role are you playing in your classroom? Are you a sage on the stage or a facilitator? Are you both?

   _____
   _____
   _____
   _____

2. How do you currently meet the learning needs of all your students? Do you work with them individually or in small groups?

_____

_____

_____

_____

Depending on your responses to these two questions, you may be able to add some new instructional strategies to your tutoring or teaching repertoire to increase student achievement in the classroom.

The Role of a Teacher as the Tutor in the Classroom

In the classroom, a teacher should not only teach content but should have a tutoring system in place. Since you are the classroom tutor, students should be allowed to freely ask questions. They must be trained, however. There are three rules that must be established, for example, in order to help all students with their studies. These rules are the following:

1. Ask four other students in the classroom before the teacher. (Used during class)

2. Got a question? Stick it! (Used during group or tutoring time)

3. Raise your hand, and I'll call on you. (Used during instruction)

The first rule should be used each day and modeled. It is important to model positive expectations so that students can ask questions about asking three students before the teacher. This rule means that any student should ask any three students in the classroom, preferably near his or her desk.

This rule is intended to build on the concept of a "learning community." Research shows that students learn from each other, and oftentimes students may be able to recall information based upon something their peers have said. The bottom line is that students should be comfortable asking and receiving help from their peers. This method is highly effective if used appropriately. This message should be conveyed to parents from the onset so that they are aware of the system. Please understand that you should not rely solely on this method, since you are the teacher of record in the classroom. For example, my second year of implementing the procedures for asking questions, I assumed that all the students understood the procedures, but I quickly realized that students and parents did not understand the rationale for why students had to learn specific procedures for asking their teacher to help them.

Please be cautious when communicating this rule to both students and parents. One school year, I did not attend open house at the beginning of the school year, and many parents were skeptical about the methods (classroom procedures) that were being implemented. Most parents reported (to me) that they wanted to meet me to "get a feel" about me. Luckily, I checked out as an appropriate teacher for their child—imagine that!

A lesson learned from this experience is to communicate with parents about any new methods. For instance, I explained to the parents that their children were highly capable of learning the course material. Furthermore, I voiced my concern about teaching social skills and how important it is now, as well as for their children's future. It's one thing to have an intelligent person working in the workforce, but it's a powerful and wonderful thing to have intelligent people who are compassionate and selfless to better humankind. Once this has been communicated to parents, there is plenty of parental support, which helps with the student support in the classroom. Again, please be cautious and understand that there will be challenges, but the best recommendation is to be well versed in your classroom procedures and proactive in communicating classroom expectations. Once expectations have been communicated, it's time to implement the in-class tutoring method.

In-Class Tutoring Method

In-class tutoring is an instructional method that I have used since my second year of teaching. I experimented with this method in an elementary setting for two academic years and later refined the process to use at the middle school level. In-class tutoring is a form of tutoring that occurs in class at least twice a week. This type of tutoring requires that teachers plan ahead and have a good command of the subjects in which they teach. In-class tutoring can occur in either small groups or individually. In my experience, this method works best with groups no larger than five students.

How Is In-Class Tutoring Structured?

In-class tutoring is structured so that between four and six students is seen on a daily basis, depending on their needs. Three steps are involved:

1. Create an in-class tutoring schedule.
2. Develop in-class tutoring groups.
3. Determine eligibility guidelines for students who need in-class tutoring.

By creating an in-class tutoring schedule, one is able to plan the days that tutoring will be offered. For example, I would host in-class tutoring on Tuesdays, Wednesdays, and Thursdays.

Below is an example of my tutoring schedule.

Tuesdays	Wednesdays	Thursdays
Periods 1/2	Periods 2/3	Periods 6/7
Group 1	**Group 1**	**Group 1**
Student A	Student A	Student A
Student B	Student B	Student B
Student C	Student C	Student C
Student D	Student D	Student D
Group 2	**Group 2**	**Group 2**
Student E	Student E	Student E
Student F	Student F	Student F
Student G	Student G	Student G
Student H	Student H	Student H
Group 3	**Group 3**	**Group 3**
Student I	Student I	Student I
Student J	Student J	Student J
Student K	Student K	Student K
Student L	Student L	Student L

You will notice that I had to code which groups contained what type of students. For instance, Group 1 is for students who scored 60-65 percent on their quiz on solving proportions. Group 2 is composed of students who scored 70-75 percent on their quiz on solving proportions. Group 3 is for students who scored 80-85 percent on their quiz on solving proportions, and Group 4 is for students who scored 50 percent or below. This group will require a great deal of assistance. These groups were formed based upon performance on the quiz rather than mathematical ability. It's important to focus on performance because students need to focus on their weaknesses to improve overall achievement. It's not always a good idea to group students according to mathematical ability when conducting in- tutoring sessions. Please remember that as the chief learner of record you should inform students (and parents) that in-class tutoring will occur, and what the student expectations are within the classroom.

Tracking Students' Progress during In-Class Tutoring

In-class tutoring requires that the teacher tracks the student's progress.

Given that students will be working in groups of between four and six, it may be a good idea to assign numerical grades and provide a summary (three to five sentences) on each student. Below is an example about working on equivalent fractions, improper fractions, and mixed numbers:

1. **Student A:** Student A worked on equivalent fractions. He needs more assistance with finding equivalent fractions. Student A scored 80 percent. Prior to working on equivalent fractions, we attempted to work on generating a mixed number equivalent to a given improper fraction; he said that he had forgotten equivalent fractions.

2. **Student B:** Student B worked on factors, common factors, and greatest common factor (GCF). This is a skill that will be forthcoming in class. Student B had a good conceptual understanding of what factors, common factors, and GCF really are. When a larger number was given, for which she was to find the GCF, she was not as confident. Therefore we will address factors, common factors, and GCF for the next two sessions to ensure that Student B truly understands.

While this seems time consuming, it provides rich data that no standardized test could ever give, because this information is recorded in real time. This method is ideal for smaller classes. It can, however, be implemented in large classes—it just takes some thought and a rotating schedule.

If this is being implemented in a large class, the teacher could implement the following organizational systems:

1. File-folder system with each student's name
2. Five-subject notebook to record notes (one section for each class period) with each page dedicated to a student
3. Preprinted template to help with note-taking

Any method works with in-class tutoring, but my favorite is the second method. This method is my favorite because it is mobile, and you can take it home with you and type the notes, if you wish. I typically typed notes only for students whose parents requested teacher conferences. This was concrete evidence, along with numerical grades, to justify why their child had received a particular grade in class. Other purposes for which these methods are great include special education and failure documentation. Parents are less prone to challenging mounds of documentation. In fact, they will support you because they know that you truly care about their child's education. As a private tutor, you have the competitive advantage in this situation because this strategy is not new to you. In any event, the paper trail is time consuming, but when you weigh the benefits . . . all parties involved have won—what's better than that?

> **EXPERT'S ADVICE:** The in-class tutoring method will help you improve your tutoring skills. If you are thinking about becoming a private tutor, then this is a great opportunity for you to help build your skills. Most importantly, your students are benefitting from the one-on-one assistance.
>
> I recommend that you get to know your students first by administering both a learning styles inventory and a multiple intelligence survey to see how to help your students. Once you have done this, you can implement in-class tutoring groups. Typically, this is done in early October through the end of the school year. As you begin working with students, you will quickly realize that students will show progress and groups will need to be changed. The most important concept to realize is that good teaching includes tutoring.

Peer Tutoring in the Classroom

Another type of tutoring that has been around for some time now but is needed in the twenty-first-century classroom is the peer tutoring method. According to Miller (2005):

In today's classrooms, it is becoming increasingly difficult to distinguish the special education students from the regular education students. With the No Child Left Behind Act and the increased expectancy for inclusion of all students in the regular school population, teachers are finding themselves in classrooms of diverse learners, including students with emotional/behavior disorders (EBD) (p. 25).

Peer tutoring is an instructional strategy that I have used heavily at the middle school level. In my middle school advanced classes, there are anywhere from thirty to thirty-five students enrolled in class. In my classroom, I purposefully allow students to choose their own groups for two reasons: (1) to determine whether these students can work together and (2) to build a sense of community in the classroom. Students are usually anxious about their new class and having them in this type of arrangement will reduce anxiety. Also, students sit in this arrangement for about two weeks, which gives me plenty of time to collect rich data on how the students in each class learn and interact with each other. Toward the end of the two-week period, students practice how to work with their peers in a structured learning environment. For instance, students typically work in groups of three or four and each student has a role in the group.

Research shows that peer tutoring has value to students. According to Miller (2005), "The benefits of peer tutoring for students—regardless of disability or functioning—are: (a) higher academic achievement; (b) improved relationships with peers; (c) improved personal and social development; and (d) increased motivation" (p. 27). Peer tutoring is a research-based instructional method and should be used in the classroom often.

Structure of Peer Tutoring in the Classroom

There are many different ways that teachers can use peer tutoring in the classroom, but the most effective is Group Peer Tutoring (GPT). Group Peer Tutoring is a method of peer tutoring in which students of the same or similar age assist each other during a class period as either a whole group or in small groups. For different units, students are placed in groups at random or strategically. When implementing this instructional method, it's imperative that classroom policies and procedures are in place. The best way to ensure that students are compliant and will follow classroom procedures is by allowing students to come up with the group norms when working in groups. You will be amazed at how critical students are of each other.

Miller (2005) offers ten steps to use when implementing peer tutoring within the classroom:

1. Define the tutoring context.
2. Define the objectives.
3. Define the curriculum area.
4. Select and match participants.
5. Identify the tutoring technique and the student contact specifics.
6. Select the tutoring materials.
7. Train the tutor(s).
8. Monitor the tutoring process and assess student learning.
9. Evaluate the program.
10. Provide feedback (p. 27).

Steps one through five should be thoroughly planned, as they will determine the resources and strategies used for the rest of the steps. The structure of peer tutoring will determine how your classroom is set up and the size of the classroom. For example, the first year that I used GPT there were desks in my classroom, and it took some creative thinking to put thirty to thirty-five desks into groups of three or four. Over time, I learned to request tables in my classroom. Of course, tables were not always available, but you are sure to get them if you use all your resources, including: (1) asking the custodian (in a nice way) to look out for tables, (2) trading unwanted furniture for pieces of furniture that are friendlier to tutoring, and (c) signing up for furniture that will be available after teachers have changed classrooms or resigned from their teaching position.

Peer tutoring is cost-effective and allows teachers to use the same resources used in other forms of tutoring. If you are creative and have some experience in designing instruction, your students will benefit from tailor-made lessons. If you are a private tutor, you have the competitive advantage in designing tailor-made lessons and delivering them in such a way that students are able to learn the material and retain it. How can one teacher ensure that all students are learning the material? Between in-class tutoring and peer tutoring, students should be able to get their needs met in the classroom.

> **EXPERT'S ADVICE:** The peer tutoring method is another instructional strategy that will take a lot of planning and preparation. Let me be very clear that this is not like cooperative grouping. You must be strategic about assigning students to work together. If you do not plan well, this strategy will be difficult to implement.

Using Online Tutoring in the Classroom

Online tutoring is a form of tutoring that has been around for more than ten years. According to Cigale (2010), "Online tutoring lets students meet with a tutor anytime, from any computer, without ever needing to make an appointment," (para. 7). There has not been a great deal of research, if any, conducted on implementing online tutoring in the classroom. Most forms of online tutoring are used in the private sector by tutors or tutoring companies. In fact, tutoring companies are now selling products to school districts for student use. As another way to reach out to my students, I offer online tutoring as an option for students who need assistance with homework or certain skills. As with any new process, there are steps to implementing online tutoring as an option in the classroom:

Step 1:
Poll the members of the class on whether they are interested in online tutoring.

Step 2:
Create a sign-up and parent permission form to inform them of the new service.

Step 3:
Host a session for students to see how it works.

Step 4:
Establish regular days and times for tutoring sessions.

Step 5:
Seek feedback from students about each session.

Let me share with you how I have used online tutoring in my classroom. First, I gave an example of how it would be cool to teach fractions online to students. The students responded, "I wish that I could learn this stuff online and did not have to come to school." That was the perfect opportunity to tell them about online tutoring, and in no time students signed up. The following day I sent home parent information and permission forms so that parents were aware of the new strategy and could give their child permission to receive online tutoring.

The sign-up sheet should be designed so that you have enough information to determine whether students would benefit from this type of tutoring. It's important that parents ask the following questions:

1. Will there need to be parental supervision?
2. Will online tutoring be free for their child?
3. Do I need to fill out a parental permission form for my child to participate?

Some parents may wonder why online-tutoring is offered, while other parents may be curious about this form of tutoring. The best solution to this issue is to ask that parents be present at the online tutoring sessions. Their presence could mean simply walking near the computer monitor so that they can witness what their child is accomplishing through online tutoring with their classroom teacher.

The first session was simply used to introduce students to the online classroom and show them how to use the various tools to communicate with me. I also showed them how I could upload worksheets and videos to enhance our learning experience. Now, are you wondering where I found this online classroom? I found an online classroom for free on www.wiziq.com. Wiziq allows one to have a free account, but academic teachers can upgrade to premium benefits without paying a dime during special promotions at the beginning of the school year, as a new-customer incentive, or for a New Year's sale. The basic version, however, will suffice. The good thing about hosting online tutoring on sites like Wiziq is that it gives tutors (or instructors) the ability to control who can enter the classroom. In fact, the tutor (or instructor) must invite the clients by sending them an e-mail using one of the following e-mail domains: (1) Yahoo, (2) Google, (3) AOL, or (4) Hotmail.

If you have online tutoring experience, you know how rewarding and effective this perk can be. Another perk in tutoring online is that if students do not attend the session, you can resume your responsibilities at home or wherever! By contrast, hosting after-school tutorials when students do not show can be costly as you may have paid for extra childcare (if you have children), used more gas to get home because of rush-hour traffic, or lost valuable time planning and prepping for the next day's lesson. In any event, online tutoring is just another way to help students in the classroom, and it can truly be rewarding.

> **EXPERT'S ADVICE:** This is a great way to address diverse learning needs and help students who may not be able to stay after-school. The one thing that must be clear is that you are providing FREE assistance, just as you would do if you were tutoring in the classroom.
>
> If you plan on becoming a private tutor, I highly recommend that you select students outside of both your school and school district. You do not want to put yourself in a situation that can be viewed as a conflict of interest. Other than that, I wish you success on implementing tutoring in your classroom.
>
> Happy Tutoring!

Now you have many strategies that will help you launch your tutoring business or add to your teaching repertoire in the classroom. Remember that there are other opportunities for you to supplement your tutoring business. You need to search for jobs and clients constantly in order to keep your tutoring business running smoothly.

There will be times when you may decide that tutoring is too much, especially if you are already working a full-time job. Life may simply get in the way, and you may have to take a break. A Chinese proverb says, "There are two kinds of job a man can do—the one he loves and the one he does best. If they're both the same, he's truly blessed." You need to keep the faith in your dreams. Best of luck and may the spirit be with you!

Where to Go From Here

Look out for other Dr. Alicia Holland's products and services. You can stay updated by visiting her personal website, www.dr-holland.com. You can also contact her via the contact form on her personal website to request services.

Should you have questions or comments, suggestions for future material, or tips, feel free to email her at: drhollandj@thetutoroutreach.com.

Join our Membership Group

Visit www.becomingabettertutorblog.com to gain access to exclusive content and interact with Dr. Alicia Holland so that you can strategically move your tutoring business from good to great.

Last but not least, if you are interested in networking with like-minded tutor business owners, join our FREE Closed Facebook Group—Becoming a Better Tutor.

Our Closed Facebook Group is growing fast and group members are eager to connect with you and share their tutoring experiences with you. We truly have what you would call a Professional Learning Community.

Until next time, Happy Tutoring!

REFERENCES

ATA (American Tutoring Association). 2012. About ATA. Retrieved August 6, 2012, from http://www.americantutoringassociation.org/

ATP (Association for the Tutoring Profession). 2012. The history of the Association for the Tutoring Profession. Retrieved August 6, 2012, from http://www.myatp.org/

Bray M. and Silova, I. (2006). The private tutoring phenomenon: international patterns and perspectives, Education in a Hidden Marketplace: Monitoring of Private Tutoring, Overview and Country Reports. Open Society Institute, New York.

Business Dictionary (2012). Cash flow. Retrieved August 19, 2012, from http://www.businessdictionary.com/definition/cash-flow.html

Constandse, R. (2012). Writing a compelling vision statement. Retrieved August 18, 2012, from http://jobfunctions.bnet.com/abstract. aspx?docid=341689

Cigale, G. 2010. Online tutoring: Just in time support. School Administrator, 67(2), 46. Retrieved August 19, 2012, from ProQuest Education Journals. (Document ID: 1950191331).

EIA (Education Industry Association). 2012. Overview of the education industry association. Retrieved August 6, 2012, from http://www. educationindustry.org/tier.asp?sid=1

Gay, L. R., & Airasian, P. 2003. *Educational research: Competencies for analysis and applications. 7th ed.* New Jersey: Pearson Education.

Gonzalez-Mena, J. 2009. *Child, family, and community: Family-centered early care and education.* Upper Saddle River, NJ: Pearson.

Gordon, E. 2009. Five ways to improve tutoring programs. Phi Delta Kappan, 90(6), 440-445. Retrieved August 14, 2012, from ProQuest Education Journals. (Document ID: 1645973011).

Harootunian, J., and Quinn, R. 2008. Identifying and describing tutor archetypes: The pragmatist, the architect, and the surveyor. The Clearing House, 82(1), 15-19.

ITA (International Tutoring Association). 2012. About ITA. Retrieved August 6, 2012, from http://www.itatutor.org/about.php

McKeachie, W. J. & Svinicki, M. (2006). Teaching tips. (12th ed.). Boston, MA: Houghton Milin Company.

Merriam-Webster Online Dictionary. 2012. What is tutoring? Retrieved July 27, 2012, from http://www.merriamwebster.com/dictionary/tutoring

Merriam-Webster Online Dictionary. 2012. Definition of praise. Retrieved June 26, 2012, from http://www.merriam-webster.com/dictionary/ praise

Miller, M. 2005. Using peer tutoring in the classroom: Applications for students with emotional/behavioral disorders. Beyond Behavior, 15(1), 25-30.

Morrison, G. R., Ross, S. M., and Kemp, J. E. 2007. Designing efective instruction. 5th ed. Hoboken, NJ: John Wiley & Sons, Inc.

NTA (National Tutoring Association). 2012. Welcome to NTA. Retrieved August 6, 2012, from http://www.ntatutor.com/

Robbins, S. & Coulter, M. (2010). Management. 9th ed. Upper Saddle River, NJ: Prentice Hall.

Robbins, S., and DeCenzo, D. 2007. Supervision today! Upper Saddle River, NJ: Prentice Hall.

Appendices

APPENDIX A:
Sample Professional Tutoring Résumé

Destiny Johnson
123 Inspiration Drive
Purpose, TX 512-111-1111
drdj@youre-maildomain.com

Objective

I am seeking to obtain a position as a professional tutor. This position will allow me to use my expertise in mathematics and teaching others.

Doctor of Education

Nova Southeastern University, Fort Lauderdale, FL 2010

Specialization: **Organizational Leadership**

Minor: **Curriculum Development**

Dissertation: "Increasing Student Achievement in Grades 6-8 Mathematics through Constructivist Instructional Strategies"

Master of Education

Northwestern State University, Natchitoches, LA 2006

Specialization: **Early Childhood Education**

Thesis: "How does participating in the ASPIRE (Achieving Success through Parental Involvement, Reading, and Education) after-school program affect the emotional domain of Hispanic students?"

Bachelor of Arts

Northwestern State University, Natchitoches, LA 2004

Specialization: **Elementary Education**

Teaching/Tutoring Certifications

Special Education in Texas, EC-12 2009

English as a Second Language (ESL) in Texas, EC-12 2009

Generalist (all subjects) in Texas, EC-4 2005

Generalist (all subjects) in Texas, 4-8 2004

Tutoring Certification as Academic Coach 2004

First Aid/AED/CPR Certification 2004-2010

Teaching Experience

Fifth Grade Generalist Teacher 2005-2007

Name of School, City

- Developed lesson plans that were aligned with best practice strategies and the different learning modalities. Also, used compacting and differentiation to meet individual student needs.
- Served as skilled facilitator in leading parent conferences.
- Served as co-team leader of our fifth-grade team of four teachers.

- Used data collection to identify individual student needs.
- 2005-2006 school year: 91% of my 5th graders passed the Texas Assessment of Knowledge and Skills (TAKS) in both Reading and Mathematics.
- 2006-2007 school year: 94% of my 5th graders passed the Texas Assessment of Knowledge and Skills (TAKS) in both Reading and Mathematics.
- Developed and implemented individual intervention plans and preventive measures for at-risk students, using data collection.
- Served as a mentor for new teachers to fifth grade.
- Developed and implemented individualized behavior plans for at-risk students using data collection.
- Modeled math demonstration lessons and engaged in curriculum development for our district math curriculum.
- Engaged in curriculum development for our district science curriculum.

Community Involvement

- **Volunteer Mentor for Youth Advocate Program**, Travis County, Austin, TX 2009-present

Professional Associations

- National Tutoring Association. 2010
- Association for the Tutoring Profession 2009
- American Tutoring Association 2007
- National Council of Teaching Mathematics 2004

References

Satisfied Client #1
Address

Phone Number E-mail Address

Satisfied Client#2
Address

Phone Number E-mail Address

Satisfied Client#3
Address

Phone Number E-mail Address

APPENDIX B:

Sample Tutoring Services Registration Form (Child Client Version)

Name of Your Tutoring Business

TUTORING SERVICES REGISTRATION FORM

To help us meet all of your child's educational needs, please fill out the front and back of this form completely and accurately.

CHILD'S INFORMATION:

Name: _____

Birth Date: _____ Age: _____ Sex: ❏ F ❏ M

Address: _____

City: _____ State: _____ ZIP: _____

Home telephone #: _____ Other #: _____

E-mail: _____

Do other siblings live in the home? ❏ No ❏ Yes If yes, please list their names: _____
_____

Whom may we thank for referring you to our office? ❏ website
❏ Tutors Teach ❏ Friend ❏ Relative ❏ Phone book ❏ Walk-in
❏ Other _____

PARENT/GUARDIAN INFORMATION:

❏ Father ❏ Stepfather ❏ Guardian

Name: _____ DOB: _____

Employer: _____ Work #: _____

Home telephone #: _____ Cell #: _____

❏ Father ❏ Stepfather ❏ Guardian

Name: _____ DOB: _____

Employer: _____ Work #: _____

Home telephone #: _____ Cell #: _____

EDUCATIONAL HISTORY:

Why is your child here today? _____

Is this your child's first visit to a tutor? ❏ Yes ❏ No

If no, date of last visit: _____

Current school name: _____

School district: _____

Current grade level: _____ Teacher(s): _____, _____

How does your child like to learn? Check all that apply:

❏ listening to others ❏ looking at pictures or visuals

❏ hands-on learning ❏ movement

Does your child have a learning disability? ❏ Yes ❏ No

Please describe: _____

Does your child have an Individualized Educational Plan (IEP)? ❏ Yes ❏ No

If so, please provide a copy of it to our office to better assist your child. You may fax it to 512-233-5389 or e-mail to your e-mail address@yourdomain.com

Has your child ever been home schooled? ❏ Yes ❏ No Please describe:

Has your child been retained in school? If so, at which grade level(s)?

Has your child failed a state assessment? If so, at which grade level(s)?

Place a check in the box below if your child has or had any of the following problems:

❑ learning disability ❑ lack of self-confidence

❑ turning assignments in late or missing assignments

❑ lack of study skills ❑ lack of motivation ❑ test anxiety

MEDICAL HISTORY

Is your child in good general health? ❑ Yes ❑ No

If no, please describe: _____

Were there any problems at birth? ❑ Yes ❑ No

If yes, please describe: _____

Are your child's immunizations and booster shots up-to-date? ❑ Yes ❑ No

Has your child ever been allergic to anything? ❑ Yes ❑ No

What was the drug/food and type of reaction? _____

Has your child had any surgical operations? ❑ Yes ❑ No

If yes, what? _____

Has your child ever been hospitalized? ❑ Yes ❑ No

If yes, for what? _____

CURRENT MEDICATIONS

Name/Strength (mg) How often? Reason taken

_____
_____
_____

SOCIAL HISTORY

Does your child have problems with any of the following?

❑ speech ❑ hearing ❑ vision ❑ sleep

Do you consider your child to be?

❑ advanced learning ❑ progressing normally ❑ a slow learner

Child's first language? _____

Second language? _____

Is your child adopted? ❏ Yes ❏ No If yes, what age? _____

Child's favorites (pet, toy, color, friend, hobby, etc.) _____

How does your child view learning? _____

AUTHORIZATION AND RELEASE:

I understand that payment is due before services are rendered, and I agree to be responsible for payment of all services rendered on behalf of my dependent(s). I understand that any unpaid balances may be sent to a collection company and that the debtor is responsible for all collection charges. I understand that all tutoring sessions that are not canceled twenty-four hours before their scheduled time will incur a regular tutoring session fee.

To the best of my knowledge, the questions on this form have been accurately answered. I understand that providing incorrect information can affect my child's instructional plan and the way that my child is taught. It is my responsibility to inform the tutoring office of any changes in my child's medical status. I authorize YOUR TUTORING BUSINESS NAME to release any information, including the diagnosis and records of any tutoring sessions or examination rendered to my child during the period of his or her tutoring needs with YOUR TUTORING BUSINESS NAME.

Signature of parent/guardian: _____

Date: _____

Printed name: _____

Relationship: _____

APPENDIX C:

Sample Tutoring Services Registration Form (Adult Client Version)

Name of Your Tutoring Business

TUTORING SERVICES REGISTRATION FORM

To help us meet all of your educational needs, please fill out the front and back of this form completely and accurately.

CLIENT INFORMATION:

Name: _____

Birth Date: _____ Age: _____ Sex: ❑ F ❑ M

Address: _____

City: _____ State: _____ ZIP: _____

Home telephone #: _____ Other #: _____

E-mail: _____

Do other siblings live in the home? ❑ No ❑ Yes If yes, please list their names: _____
_____

Whom may we thank for referring you to our office? ❑ website
❑ Tutors Teach ❑ Friend ❑ Relative ❑ Phone book ❑ Walk-in
❑ Other _____

EDUCATIONAL HISTORY:

Why are you here today? _____

Is this your first visit to a tutor? ❑ Yes ❑ No

If no, date of last visit: _____

Current school/College name: _____

Circle One: Undergraduate or Graduate

Program of study: _____

When will you graduate? _____

How do you like to learn? Check all that apply:

❑ listening to others   ❑ looking at pictures or visuals

❑ hands-on learning   ❑ movement

Do you have a learning disability?   ❑ Yes ❑ No Please describe:

Do you have an Individualized Educational Plan (IEP)?   ❑ Yes ❑ No

If so, please provide a copy of it to our office to better assist you. You may fax it to 512-233-5389 or e-mail to your e-mail address@yourdomain.com

Have you ever been home schooled?   ❑ Yes ❑ No Please describe:

Have you been retained in school? If so, at which grade level(s)?

Have you failed a state assessment? If so, at which grade level(s)?

Place a check in the box below if you have or had any of the following problems:

❑ Learning disability   ❑ lack of self-confidence

❑ turning assignments in late or missing assignments

❑ lack of study skills   ❑ lack of motivation

MEDICAL HISTORY

Are you in good general health? ❑ Yes ❑ No

If no, please describe: _____

Were there any problems at birth? ❑ Yes ❑ No

If yes, please describe: _____

Are your immunizations and booster shots up-to-date? ❑ Yes ❑ No

Have you ever been allergic to anything? ❑ Yes ❑ No

What was the drug/food and type of reaction?

_____

Have you had any surgical operations? ❑ Yes ❑ No If yes, what?

_____

Have you ever been hospitalized? ❑ Yes ❑ No If yes, for what?

_____

CURRENT MEDICATIONS:

Name/Strength (mg)/How often? Reason taken:

_____
_____
_____

AUTHORIZATION AND RELEASE:

I understand that payment is due before services are rendered, and I agree to be responsible for payment of all services rendered on my behalf. I understand that any unpaid balances may be sent to a collection company and that the debtor is responsible for all collection charges. I understand that all tutoring sessions that are not canceled twenty-four hours before their scheduled time will incur a regular tutoring session fee.

To the best of my knowledge, the questions on this form have been accurately answered. I understand that providing incorrect information can affect my instructional plan and the way that I am taught. It is my responsibility to inform the tutoring office of any changes in my medical status. I authorize YOUR TUTORING BUSINESS NAME to release any information, including the diagnosis and records of any tutoring sessions or examination rendered to me during the period of my tutoring needs with YOUR TUTORING BUSINESS NAME.

Signature of client: _____ Date: _____

Printed name: _____ Relationship: _____

APPENDIX D:

Sample Tutoring Guidelines

[Your Business Name]

Tutoring Guidelines

To provide your child with the best tutoring experience, it is crucial for all parties involved to understand and uphold their responsibilities in your child's education.

To ensure that academic, legal, and ethical standards are met for tutoring purposes, the statements below must be read and agreed to before services are rendered by [Your Business Name].

The [Your Business Name] tutor will:

- be on time to meet your child for tutoring sessions;
- be prepared for each session with an engaging lesson and materials to support the student's learning needs;
- complete the prescribed number of hours each week;
- adhere to the [Your Business Name] code of ethics;
- adhere to all policies and procedures set forth at [Your Business Name].

The parent will:

- complete all necessary documentation/notification pertaining to their child's enrollment for [Your Business Name] tutoring services;

- ensure that their child is on time to the tutoring session. The [Your Business Name] tutor will only wait fifteen minutes past the scheduled meeting time for your child to arrive before canceling the tutoring session. In the event that this happens, you are still responsible for paying the session fee.
- Pay for all tutoring sessions provided through [Your Business Name].

The student will:

- participate actively, be respectful, and be held accountable within all aspects of tutoring provided through [Your Business Name].
- be prepared with the appropriate book(s), notebook, pen or pencil, and assignments;
- take responsibility for gathering his or her class assignments and test schedule in advance of the tutoring session. This will help the [Your Business Name] tutor tailor tutoring sessions to help your child succeed in his or her classes.
- complete all assignments worked on during tutoring sessions to the best of his or her ability.

_____   _____
Parent Signature   Date

_____   _____
[Your Business Name] Tutor   Date

_____
Student Signature Date

APPENDIX E:

Sample Client Policies and Procedures

[Your Business Name]

Client Policies and Procedures

Mission Statement: I am offering my services to students because I believe that success starts from within. Thus, I see my role as the facilitator for helping these young individuals strive and remain confident when working with educational activities.

Pretest Assessment: During the first session, I would like to give your child a pretest assessment on the concepts that we are exploring. This assessment will be brief and will enable us to meet your child's needs and spend quality instructional time to build upon already learned concepts.

Supplies: I will provide everything that your child needs.

Tutoring Fee: Starts at $35.00 per hour due after tutoring service has been rendered, or you may pay in advance for tutoring sessions. Please note that if I am traveling to your home, the tutoring fee will include traveling expenses. (Please note that tutoring packages are available for purchase.)

Method of Payment: You may pay by cash, check, or money order only. If paying with a check or money order, please make it payable to: [Your Business Name].

Tutoring Sessions: Tutoring sessions will be tailored to your child's needs, based upon observation, parent and child input and/or requests, in addition to the pretest assessment. Each session will have an objective.

Start/Stop Time for Sessions: Please have your child arrive five minutes before the session begins. I will wait fifteen minutes past the scheduled meeting time for your child to arrive before canceling the tutoring session. In the event that you are more than fifteen minutes late, you are still responsible for paying the session fee.

Please be back five minutes before the session ends. If you are late picking your child up from tutoring, you will be charged for a full session.

Availability: Please contact [Your Business Name] to check available times.

Cancellations: If your child is not able to meet at his or her assigned tutoring session, then I require at least twenty-four-hour notice. If I am not given twenty-four-hour notice, then you will be charged a regular tutoring session fee starting at $35.00 per hour. I recommend that you call my cell phone [Insert Your Phone Number] first. If no one answers, then leave a detailed message and a callback number. Also, you may e-mail me at youre-mailaddress@yourdomain.com. In any case, I will return provide a phone call and/or e-mail confirmation of your cancellation.

Severe Weather/Emergencies: Due to natural disaster, severe weather, or other such emergencies, tutoring sessions will be canceled and/or rescheduled. In the event that this occurs, I will contact you immediately.

If you have any further questions, then please feel free to call me at [Insert Your Phone Number] or e-mail me at your [emailaddress@yourdomain.com].

By signing below, you acknowledge that you will agree to the terms of my tutoring services:

Parent/Guardian Signature: _____

Date: _____

For Office Use Only:

Date Received: _____

Authorized Signature: _____

APPENDIX F:

Sample Instructional Plan

March 17, 2010

To the Parents of **Child's Name:**

Based on parent and child input, teacher observation, and pre-assessments, I am recommending that your child and I follow the recommended schedule listed below for the next eight sessions. After the next eight sessions, I recommend a parent-tutor conference to determine our next steps in meeting your child's needs.

SESSIONS	CONCEPTS BEING COVERED
1 [SESSION DATE AND YEAR]	• 3.1C Determine the value of a collection of coins and bills.
2 [SESSION DATE AND YEAR]	• 3.6A Identify and extend whole-number and geometric patterns to make predictions and solve problems. • 3.2C Use fraction names and symbols to describe fractional parts of whole objects or sets of objects with denominators of twelve or less.

3 [SESSION DATE AND YEAR]	• 3.7A Generate a table of paired numbers based on a real-life situation, such as insects and legs. • 3.7B Identify patterns in a table of related number pairs based on a real-life situation and extend the table.
4 [SESSION DATE AND YEAR]	• 3.8A Name, describe, and compare shapes and solids using formal geometric vocabulary.

APPENDIX G:

Sample Monitoring Notes

Monitoring Notes for Tutoring Sessions

Client's Name: _____

03/18/10 1:00 PM-2:00 PM

> **Today's Objective:** We are working on determining the value of a collection of coins and bills.
>
> **Attitude/Effort:** John Doe was engaged in the lesson and enthusiastic about learning. ☺
>
> **Progress:** Math: John Doe and I had allowance for the month. Initially, John Doe counted out $210 dollars. When we counted it together, John Doe had $272. Next, we went to identifying the coins. He doesn't recognize that he can trade out coins. For example, five nickels trade out for a quarter. In addition, John Doe needs more practice setting up addition and subtraction of money problems. This is a skill that will need additional practice and can also be used in other areas of math.

- **Reading:** John Doe did a better job in reading this time around because he proved his answers using examples from the story. John Doe is currently reading at 105 words/minute, which is right on target. At this point (spring semester), John Doe should be reading at 110 words/minute.

- **How you can help at home?**

  o **Math:** Allow John Doe to count money out to the cashier at the store. Also, have him predict how much he should receive from the cashier. It's important that the balances are not larger than $20.00, as he still needs practice with this. Once he has mastered this skill, however, he should be challenged with larger balances.

- **Reading:** John Doe needs to read on a daily basis to increase his fluency. He tends to omit words more often than inserting additional words when reading. Also, if there's a word that is unfamiliar to him, he tends to substitute for it a word that is familiar to him. Exposing him to various grade level texts will help him with both his fluency and vocabulary.

- **NEXT STEPS:** Our next two sessions are slated for Wednesday, March 24, 2010, at 4:20 PM and Thursday, March 25, 2010, at 4:20 p.m. If he will be attending only one session, please let me know which day so that I can readjust his instructional plan and plan accordingly.

APPENDIX H:

Sample Teacher's Online Tutoring Sign-Up Form

Directions: Please print your name and add your e-mail account below so that I can register you for an online tutoring session. Also, please indicate your preferred time and whether you have access to a computer for a session. (Note: All sessions are free!)

Name	E-mail Account	Preferred time (PM Only)	Computer Access?	New to Online Tutoring?
		6:00 or 7:00	Y or N	Y or N
		6:00 or 7:00	Y or N	Y or N
		6:00 or 7:00	Y or N	Y or N
		6:00 or 7:00	Y or N	Y or N

Index

A

Accounting system, 81
Accounts payable and accounts receivable, 83
Additional practice after tutoring sessions, 172–174
Adult learners
    architect tutors, 143–146
    pragmatist tutors, 141–142
    registration form, 202–204
    surveyor tutors, 146–147
    tutoring archetypes that work best, 140–147
Advertising, 56–66. *See also* Promoting your business
    local advertising, 58–59
    online, 58
AED (Automated external defibrillator) certification, résumé information, 32
American Tutoring Association (ATA), 20
Archetypes of tutors, 149–150
    architect tutors, 143–146
    pragmatists, 141–142
    surveyor tutors, 146–147
Architect tutors, 143–146
Article writing, to supplement income, 98
Assessing your strengths and weaknesses, 27–30
Assessments
    needs assessments, 115–121
    part of framework for effective tutoring, 150
    pre-assessments, 118–123
    progress-monitoring assessments, 124–125
Association for the Tutoring Profession (ATP), 20–21
Association of Educators in Private Practice (AEPP), 19
Attitude/effort component of monitoring notes, 166–168
Attracting clients. *See* Promoting your business
Authorization to release information form, 50

B

Baseline assessment, 116
Birthdays of clients, remembering, 87–88
Bookkeeping basics, 81–84
Business checking account, 76–77
Business forms. *See* Forms
Business licenses and permits, 40–41
Business plan, 40
    location and hours of operation, 41–44
    writing proposals, to supplement income, 100

C

Cash expenditures, records, 82
Cash flow, 80–81
Certifications, résumé information, 32, 195
Chamber of Commerce membership, 63
Checking account, 76–77
Class schedule and setting goals, 129
Classroom tutoring, 176–190
    asking other students before the teacher, 177–178
    in-class tutoring method, 179–183
    online tutoring, 186–189, 214
    peer tutoring, 183–186
    role of tutor, 176–177
    teacher as tutor, 177–179
Clients
    conflicts, handling, 88–89
    consultations with, 109–114
    following up with regularly, 86–87
    inappropriate questions of, 112–113
    maintaining good relationship with, 85–89
    nonpayment, handling, 89
    policies and procedures document, 52–54, 207–209
    postcards, sending, 87–88
    referral system, 93–94
    tutoring guidelines for, 49–50, 205–206
    tutoring interviews with parents, 107–109
    your best clients, 105–107
Closing tutoring sessions, 152–154
College students as tutors, 23–24
Colorful and vibrant environment, 45–46
Competition, researching, 69
Conflicts with clients, handling, 88–89
Consultations, 109–114
    inappropriate questions of clients, 112–113
    "too expensive" claims of parents, 110–111

Contact information, website page, 62–63
Content knowledge of tutors, 149
Contract, policies and procedures document as, 52–54, 207–209
CPR certification, résumé information, 32
Credit rating, 77–80
Curriculum writing, 99
Cutting expenses, 89–92

D

Data collection to determine tutoring needs, 117–118
Degreed professionals as tutors, 23, 25
Demand for tutoring services, 17–18
Direct mailing, 63
Discounts for client referrals, 93–94
Documentation. *See also* Forms; Recordkeeping
    monitoring notes, 163–170, 212–213

E

Economically uncertain times
    client referral system, 93–94
    cutting expenses, 89–92
    maintaining good relationship with clients, 85–89
    special promotions, 92–94
    supplementing your tutoring income, 94–102
Education
    higher education, working towards, 101–102
    résumé information, 32, 194–195
Education Industry Association (EIA), 19
Effort/attitude component of monitoring notes, 166–168
EIA (Education Industry Association), 19
E-mail
    advertising, 64–65
    to cut expenses, 89–90
Environment for tutoring, 45–48
    colorful and vibrant, 45–46
    engaging opportunities, 46
    inspiring messages, 47
    lighting, 45
    office design, 47
Expenses, cutting, 89–92
    e-mailing, 89–90
    printing only what you need, 90–91
    recycling office supplies, 91–92
Experience, résumé section, 32, 195–196

Expert's Advice
  accounting systems, 83
  architect tutors, 145–146
  beginning and ending tutoring sessions, 154
  business plans, 40
  client referral system, 94
  content knowledge, building, 101
  data collection to assess client's needs, 117–118
  electronic form *vs.* paper, 92
  framework for effective tutoring, 151
  gifts and gift cards as rewards, 162–163
  good credit, importance of, 79–80
  homework tutor's access to grades, 135
  hours of operation, 44
  inappropriate questions asked by clients, 113
  in-class tutoring method, 183
  instructional plans, 124
  last-minute strategic tutoring for college test, 140
  loans, obtaining, 79
  marketing strategies, 60
  monitoring notes, 165, 170
  nonpayment, handling, 107
  office, 48
  online classroom tutoring, 189
  peer tutoring, 186
  practice packets, 174
  pragmatist tutors, 142
  praising students, 158
  pre-assessments, 120–121, 122–123
  pricing, 69, 72, 73, 74
  professional tutoring association, choosing, 21
  progress-monitoring assessments, 125
  promoting your business, 66
  tickets, using as rewards, 160–161
  time cards for tutoring sessions, 172
  "too expensive" claims of parents, how to handle, 111
  vision and mission statements, 39
  website, 66
  worksheets, use of, 145–146

F

Fees. *See also* **Pricing**
  consultation fees, 109–110
  tutoring fees, 67–74

Finances, 76–84
    accounting system, 81
    bookkeeping basics, 81–84
    business checking account, 76–77
    cash flow, 80–81
    credit rating and, 77–80
    cutting expenses, 89–92
    good credit, 77–80
    nonpayment, handling, 89, 105–106
    questions to consider, 76
    records, 82–83
    supplementing your tutoring income, 94–102
First aid certification, résumé information, 32
Flat-rate tutoring, 74
Forms, 49–54
    authorization to release information, 50
    client policies and procedures, 52–54, 207–209
    guidelines for tutors, parents, and clients, 49–50, 205–206
    interviews with parents, bringing to, 108
    release from liability, 50
    sample forms, 194–214
    tutoring services registration form, 49, 198–204
Framework for effective tutoring, 148–151
Freelance writing, to supplement income, 97–100

G

Gifts and gift cards as rewards, 161–163
    education-related, 162
    inexpensive, 161–162
    timeframe, 162
Goals, setting, 125–130
    class schedule and, 129
    interview questions, 126–130
    plans after high school, 127
    school year goals, 126–127
    student involvement in setting, 126, 127, 130
    tutor's assistance in meeting goals, 129
Good credit rating, attaining, 77–80
Grades, tutor's access to, 133–134
Grant writing, to supplement income, 100
Green, money-saving practices, 89–92
Group tutoring sessions, 22–23
Guidelines for tutors, parents, and clients, 49–50, 205–206

H

High school learners
    architect tutors, 143–146
    pragmatist tutors, 141–142
    surveyor tutors, 146–147
    tutoring archetypes that work best, 140–147
High school seniors as tutors, 23–25
Home office design, 48
Homework tutors, 132–135
Hours of operation, 41–44

I

In-class tutoring method, 179–183
    how structured, 179–181
    schedule, 179–181
    tracking students' progress, 181–183
Income opportunities to supplement tutoring earnings, 94–102
    article writing, 98
    curriculum writing, 99
    freelance writing, 97
    grant writing, 100
    substitute teaching, 95–97
    technical writing, 98
Individualized tutoring sessions, 22–23
Inspiring messages, 47
Instructional plans, 123–124
    monitoring notes component, 168–169
    sample, 210–211
Instructional tutors, 135–137
International Tutoring Association (ITA), 20
Internet. *See* **Online activities and resources**
Interviews
    goal-setting questions, 126–130
    tutoring interviews with parents, 107–109
Introduction of tutoring session
    assessing your strengths and weaknesses, 27–30
    chances for success, 30–31
    finding your niche, 30–31
    résumé, crafting, 31–33
Introduction to tutoring, 17–33
    demand for tutoring services, 17–18
    professional associations, 18–21
    types of tutoring, 22–23
    who can tutor, 23–26
Inventory records, 83
ITA (International Tutoring Association), 20

L

"Learning community," developing in the classroom, 178
Liability release form, 50
Licensed pre- and post-assessments, 121–122
Licenses (business), 40–41
Lighting, 45
Loans, obtaining, 77–79
Location of business, 41–42

M

Mailings, 63
    postcards, 87–88
Marketing strategies, 56–66
    advanced, 60–66
    advertising, 58–59
    basic, 58–60
    Chamber of Commerce membership, 63
    direct mailing, 63
    e-mail advertising, 64–65
    instructional tutor's plan, 136–137
    networking, 59
    promotional products, 63
    sponsorships, offering, 61
Medical information, tutoring registration form, 200, 203–204
Military veterans as tutors, 23, 25, 26
Mission and vision statements, 36–39
Money management, 76–84
Monitoring notes, 163–170
    next instructional steps, 168–169
    parent resources, 169
    parent-tutor conference requests, 169–170
    sample, 212–213
    student and session information, 166
    student progress, 168
    upcoming sessions, 169–170
Motivation, praising, 155–158

N

National Tutoring Association (NTA), 19–20
Needs assessments, 115–121
    baseline assessment, 116
    data collection, 117–118
    how to conduct, 115–118
    identifying clients' needs, 118–121
    purpose of, 116

Networking, 59
No Child Left Behind (NCLB) Act, 18, 183–184
Nonpayment, handling, 89, 105–107
NTA (National Tutoring Association), 19–20

O

Office environment, 45–47
Office supplies, recycling, 91–92
Online activities and resources
    advertising, 58
    classroom tutoring, 186–189, 214
    sign-up form for teacher's online tutoring, 214
    teaching and tutoring, to supplement income, 101
    website, developing, 61–63
Opening tutoring sessions, 151–152
Organizational skills, helping student with, 133–134

P

Package pricing, 72–73
Parents
    communicating new learning methods, 178–179
    online tutoring information, 188
    parent-tutor conference requests, 169–170
    pre-assessment information, 118–119
    resources for, in monitoring notes, 169
    "too expensive" claims, 110–111
    tutoring guidelines for, 49–50, 205–206
    tutoring interviews with, 107–109
    as tutors, 23, 25
    unacceptable actions of, dealing with, 51–52
Payment issues, handling, 89, 105–107
Pedagogy of tutor, 150
Peer tutoring in the classroom, 183–186
    benefits of, 184
    structuring, 184–186
Performance, praising, 155–158
Permits (business), 40–41
Philosophy of tutoring, developing, 34–36
Planning your business
    business plan, 40
    forms, 49–54. *See also* **Forms**.
    introduction to tutoring, 17–33
    starting and legalizing your business, 34–54
    tutoring environment, 45–48
    tutoring philosophy, 34–36
    vision and mission statements, 36–39

Policies and procedures document, 52–54, 207–209
    interviews with parents, bringing to, 108
Post-assessments, 121–123
Postcards, sending to clients, 87–88
Practice packets, 172–174
Pragmatist tutors, 141–142
Praising student motivation and performance, 155–158
Pre-assessments, 118–123
    creating your own, 120–121
    information from parents, 118–119
    information from students, 119
    licensed assessments, using, 121–122
    new clients, using with, 121
    saving for future reference, 120–121
    strategic tutoring, for, 138
Pricing, 67–74
    clients, evaluating, 71–72
    flat rate, 74
    questions to consider, 67–69
    quoting too low, 70–71
    researching the competition, 69
    strategies to boost sales, 72–74
    "too expensive" claims of parents, 110–111
    tutoring packages, 72–73
Printing only what you need, 90–91
Professional associations, 18–21
    résumé section, 33, 196
Professionals as tutors, 23, 25
Progress-monitoring assessments, 124–125
Promoting your business, 56–66
    advertising, 58–59
    basic marketing strategies, 58–60
    Chamber of Commerce membership, 63
    direct mailing, 63
    e-mail advertising, 64–65
    networking, 59
    promotional products, 63
    special promotions, 92–94
    sponsorships, offering, 61
    website, 61–63

Q

QuickBooks, 81, 83

R

Rates, setting, 67–74
Recordkeeping, 82–83
    accounts payable and accounts receivable, 83
    cash expenditures, 82
    inventory records, 83
    revenues and expenses, 82
Recycling office supplies, 91–92
References, résumé section, 33, 197
Referral system for clients, 93–94
Registration form for tutoring services, 49, 198–204
Release from liability form, 50
Release of information authorization form, 50
Résumés, 31–33, 194–197
Retirees as tutors, 23
Revenues and expenses, records, 82
Reward systems, 158–163
    gifts as rewards, 161–163
    tickets, using, 159–161

S

Sample forms
    client policies and procedures, 207–209
    instructional plans, 210–211
    monitoring notes, 212–213
    policies and procedures document, 207–209
    registration form (adult client), 202–204
    registration form (child client), 198–201
    sign-up form for teacher's online tutoring, 214
    tutoring guidelines, 205–206
Scheduling
    in-class tutoring, 179–181
    tutoring sessions and cash flow, 80–81
Skills of tutor, 150
    résumé section, 32–33
Special promotions, offering, 92–94
Sponsorships, offering, 61
State standards, 118, 123
Stay-at-home parents as tutors, 23, 25
Strategic tutors, 137–140
Strengths and weaknesses, assessing, in considering tutoring career, 27–30
Student and session information in monitoring notes, 166
Student progress
    monitoring notes, 168
    tracking, during in-class tutoring, 181–183

Students
    adult. *See* **Adult learners.**
    assessment of. *See* **Assessments.**
    monitoring notes, 163–170
    praising, 155–158
    setting goals, 125–130
    tutoring sessions. *See* **Tutoring sessions.**
Substitute teaching to supplement income, 95–97
Supplementing your tutoring income, 94–102
    article writing, 98
    curriculum writing, 99
    freelance writing, 97
    grant writing, 100
    substitute teaching, 95–97
    technical writing, 98
Surveyor tutors, 146–147

T

Teacher as tutor in the classroom, 177–179
    online tutoring, 186–189, 214
Teaching certifications, résumé section, 32, 195
Technical writing, to supplement income, 98
Tickets, using as rewards, 159–161
Time cards for tutoring sessions, 171–172
Tutor pedagogy, 150
Tutoring certifications, résumé section, 32, 195
Tutoring consultations, 109–114
Tutoring environment, 45–48
Tutoring guidelines, 49–50, 205–206
Tutoring interviews with parents, 107–109
Tutoring packages, pricing, 72–73
Tutoring philosophy, developing, 34–36
Tutoring services registration form, 49, 198–204
Tutoring sessions, 148–174
    additional practice after, 172–174
    closing, 152–154
    documenting, 163–170
    framework for effective tutoring, 148–151
    length of, 136
    monitoring notes, 163–170, 212–213
    opening, 151–152
    praising student motivation and performance, 155–158
    reward systems, 158–163
    structure of, 154–155
    time cards, 171–172

Tutors
  archetypes of, 149–150
  architect tutors, 143–146
  college students as, 23–24
  content knowledge of, 149
  high school seniors as, 23–25
  homework tutors, 132–135
  instructional tutors, 135–137
  military veterans as, 23, 25, 26
  pragmatist tutors, 141–142
  professionals as, 23, 25
  résumés, 31–33, 194–197
  retirees as, 23
  stay-at-home parents as, 23, 25
  strategic tutors, 137–140
  supplementing income, 94–102
  surveyor tutors, 146–147
  tutoring guidelines for, 49–50, 205–206
  types of, 22–23, 131–147
  who can tutor, 23–26
Types of tutoring, 22–23, 131–147
  homework tutors, 132–135
  instructional tutors, 135–137
  strategic tutors, 137–140

V

Vision and mission statements, 36–39

W

Website, developing, 61–63
Who can tutor, 23–26
Wiziq.com, 188–189
Writing, to supplement income, 97–100
  article writing, 98
  curriculum writing, 99
  grant writing, 100
  technical writing, 98

www.ingramcontent.com/pod-product-compliance
Lightning Source LLC
Chambersburg PA
CBHW070941230426
43666CB00011B/2517